Junie

Riddle

How Long Does Mourning Last

How Long Does Mourning Last

a memoir

BJ Coleman

Jariel,
Your faith inspires.
Keep it up.

BJ Coleman

Ephesians 3:14-20

Published by Deeds Publishing in Athens, GA
www.deedspublishing.com

Printed in The United States of America

Cover design by Mark Babcock. Text layout by Matt King

ISBN 978-1-947309-47-0

Books are available in quantity for promotional or premium use. For information, email info@deedspublishing.com.

First Edition, 2018

10 9 8 7 6 5 4 3 2 1

This book is dedicated to my parents, Don and Jean Cavanar, who gave permission for me to marry Dean; to Beveridge and Dale Whitlock who shared their precious son with me; to my friend Connie Hill and my cousin Darlene Woodmansee who encouraged me to write my story.

El Shaddai—God Almighty. He continues to heal my grief.

Contents

Introduction (2016)

There was not another customer in the place as I walked towards the counter where a young woman, Annabel, was working. The young woman took the ring out of the tiny envelope and I had to smile though I could feel the uninvited tears behind my eyelids. She was watching me closely as I took the ring from her hand. Then she asked me this question, "May I ask you, what the story is behind this ring?" I could tell it wasn't a general pass-the-time-of-day kind of question. I detected a concern or maybe an anxious tone in her voice. It was only a plain gold band, nothing out of the ordinary; I see them every day. She was very curious about my ring. I had left it with her sister in this small family jewelry store that morning. I asked to have a ruby added to it. They had ordered the stone for me the week before. The ring had been packed away in a box with some pictures and newspaper clippings for more than forty-eight years. This year would have been our fiftieth wedding anniversary; it was time for it to come out of hiding. Though I rarely go to the mall any more, that is where this little store is located. They had done good work for me before and were reasonably priced. I had been very apprehensive about leaving it there. It is the most precious of all my possessions. To leave it in a stranger's hands, even for just a few hours, made me anxious. I had prayed for weeks about what God wanted me to do. I asked Him to please put obstacles in my way if He didn't want me to wear it. He didn't stop me. I couldn't wait to see how it would look on my finger once again. So now it was done.

The first day I knew about or saw this golden band, fifty years ago, was the day he picked it up from another small jewelry store where he had it sized for me. He took me along to pick it up but would not let me see it. Today it looked as beautiful as the first time I saw it, shining, when he placed it on my finger. It is a wide, smooth, golden band that now has a small ruby embedded in the center. I slipped it on my finger and immediately reached for my card to pay for the service before the tears started to flow in front of this stranger. That is when Annabel asked me, "May I ask you, what the story is behind this ring? I can see it is very special to you." I hesitated; after all, she was a stranger. I was not accustomed to talking about this part of my life to anyone, much less someone I didn't know. I had been conditioned to not talk about him and to pretend that part of my life had never happened. It has taken me almost twenty years, since Sam's death, to have the courage to break out of that training. I was concerned that it would build a wall between my four children and me, but they were grown with their own families and lives, and I was alone. I guess I had kept it inside of me for so long and I just wanted to feel free to talk about him, so I answered her.

"This was my wedding band from my first husband. He was killed in the Vietnam War. It has been locked away in a box at my mother's house for more than forty-eight years. My second husband passed away almost twenty years ago, and I finally decided to take this out of hiding and wear it." I told her.

"What about the ruby?" She asked.

"It's his birthstone; he was born in July." I said. The girl smiled and just looked at me for a moment with tears in her eyes. I almost lost my composure when she whispered, "And he was the love of your life wasn't he."

I said, "Yes, he was my first love."

"Ms., you should write a book about that special love I can see in your eyes. And if you do, I want to read it." I revealed to her that I had started writing one fifteen years ago but had put it away and not written for about ten years. I told her that recently I had begun writing again and hoped I could finish it. "Please let me read your story," she pleaded with me. I promised that she could read it, if I ever finished it.

As I walked back to my car and started for home, I remembered the day I had decided to write the book. It was a few years after Sam passed away. I would not, could not, have done it while he was living. The memories came flooding back to me in living color. Every moment of time we had together was clear in my mind. After a while, I found myself agonizing over each detail and becoming depressed.

I had always turned to my writing when I was troubled or anxious about something. I had a few articles that were published in a Christian women's magazine and two of my poems were published in a book of poetry with a variety of authors. Suddenly the words just wouldn't come; eventually I lost my ability to write at all. What had happened? I had written for as long as I could remember, and now I couldn't write anything, though I tried several times in the next ten years. I was sure that my pride had gotten in the way of my words after some of my work had been published. I thought God was punishing me for that, by removing my ability.

Recently I prayed for the Lord to give me back my writing skills. Thirty-two days after that impassioned prayer, I just started writing one day on the book. I knew this would still be a very emotional undertaking, but I prayed that I had prepared myself for it.

I was cautiously starting to write again. I started slowly, and the words started to flow once more. I had no idea where this endeavor would lead me. If I could have seen into the future and what it would bring, would I have continued? I don't know, but I hope I would have had that kind of courage. I am convinced that God wanted me to write it and His timing is always perfect.

1. Texas My Texas

THOUGH IT IS A WARM OCTOBER DAY, FALL HAS ARRIVED IN TEXAS. It isn't unusual for the temperature to reach eighty degrees or more in Houston this time of year. The weather usually doesn't start to get cool until the end of October, or even November, in Southeast Texas. It is such a relief and a blessing when the scorching heat of another Texas summer is over. There are many things that I like about living in Houston, but the temperature hovering around ninety-five to over one hundred degrees with the heat index of one hundred to one hundred ten degrees or more is not one of them. The heat, humidity, and mosquitoes that come with living near the coast sometimes make summers almost unbearable if you must be outdoors. Thankfully when air conditioning became available and affordable, most people could choose to stay inside more on those sweltering days.

The work week is over, and I head for my car parked just outside the office door. I love my job as a secretary for the church where I worship, but it can be stressful and tiring at times. I open the door of my red Chevy Blazer and reach for the bright yellow, orange, and bronze silk mums lying in the back seat. I picked them up yesterday at the craft store. They look so real as I place them on the seat next to me.

I always think of my grandmother when I see flowers of any kind. She lived next door to us and, whenever we were outside, I would walk with her around the yard as she talked. Each flowerbed was filled with every kind of flowering and ornamental plant native to this area of Texas. She taught me the names of each flower and told me the varieties and unique characteristics of each one. She seemed to glow as she talked about the plants and blooms in various colors. Granny loved gladiolas, as I do, and we both loved roses. She loved one called the Peace Rose which is a variegated pink, peach, and yellow color. Though she had only a fourth-grade education, she knew the common name of each plant and the scientific name of many. I can't remember most of what she tried to teach me therefore, my gardens are not as beautiful as hers were. Though I do love fresh flowers they are not good for my mission today. The silk ones are bright and beautiful and will last much longer.

Sitting here on the busy toll road, waiting in the rush hour traffic, I feel the exhilaration I always do when the fall weather is coming. I drive with my windows open so I can enjoy the autumn in the air. Maybe it is because I was born in October that it attracts me so. Though I'm well past the age of thrill a child feels when anticipating their birthday, I guess I still hope for a happy day. I have a lot of memories of past birthdays, some good and some are not.

As the leaves begin to turn various shades of yellow, orange, and red, we know that the first cold days are near. Many people don't like the abbreviated autumns we have here in Texas, especially if they have moved here from places where the fall is identified by the seasonal months of September through November. But the delayed and subtle changes of autumn are all I have known. After all, I have lived in Texas all my life. I was born in Amarillo and my family moved to Houston when I was four.

My daughters and I have already started planning our Thanksgiving dinner. The children and I have rented a beach house in Galveston each Thanksgiving since their dad died. It seems to ease their pain of Thanksgiving memories spent with him. We all loved walking on the early morning beach or sitting on the deck of the beach house with our first cup of coffee in the morning, it's something we look forward to when we are there. We shop on the Strand near the port of Galveston for early Christmas gifts as a part of that weekend. Some of the shops have typical tourist items such as anything that can possibly be made of sea shells. But many of the establishments are unique with local artists' work, old military items, and beach wear. There is an old-time drug store where they make their own candies, ice cream, and sodas that were popular in the forties and fifties. Every year, we hope the weather will be cool for the holidays and sometimes it is. My daughter-in-law especially wishes for cold holidays; she is from West Virginia where the weather is cold enough for snow and ice. My son understands her longing and they visit her home as much as possible. He chose the perfect mate for himself. They fit together like a hand in a glove.

Very soon we will be preparing for the busy Christmas season. The hustle and bustle of people in the shopping malls will become a common sight around town and the traffic will increase. There will be lights and glittering decorations in the stores, on the streets, and in the houses. The girls love the holidays more than I do, but I enjoy watching them and my grandchildren get excited.

I love Galveston Island at any time of year. I feel my heart swell with emotion at the thought of it. The salt air that touches my senses as I drive across the causeway brings memories of the calmness and peace that is just ahead on this intriguing island. The waters there aren't often blue, nor are the beaches as beautiful as some, but I love the historic tales of the island. You can find old used bookstores in out of the way places where much Galveston history is hidden. There are ancient reports of the cannibals and pirates, of the deadly hurricane of 1900, and of the famous and infamous celebrities and organized crime bosses who frequented the island's night life in the nineteen twenties through the forties. Then there was Fort Crockett that became a POW camp during World War II. When you walk among the ruins, you can imagine the fear and misery of the men who were held there. I am fascinated by all the things there are to see or read about the island. Few places the size of Galveston have such a diverse and exciting history. Talk with me for very long and I'll have you loving Galveston, also.

Easing off the Tollway and driving through the back roads towards my destination, I can feel the breeze that promises cooler weather is coming soon. Many of the trees native to southeast Texas line this street. The area is filled with tall pine trees and the live oaks. There are so many species of evergreens that seem to enhance the appearance of our meager autumn. One of the most beautiful images to me is the lovely blue Texas sky through towering pine trees with the sunlight sparkling between the green pine needles and the pinecones as they reach heavenward.

Springtime in Texas brings fields covered with bluebonnets across the state, especially in what is called the Hill Country of central Texas. The name of these flowers perfectly describes how they look, like little blue bonnets with white tips lined up in a row on the stem. When the soft breezes blow over these fields, it brings to my mind a deep blue ocean with occasional whitecaps dancing across the tops of the waves. Some of the fields of bluebonnets are mixed with the bright red-orange Indian Paintbrushes for indescribable pictures. I have seen parts of the country that are as lovely or even more lovely as my home state, but I love my Texas.

2. Who Am I And How Did I Get Here?

I GREW UP IN THE SIMPLE TIME OF THE 1950S AND 1960S. I IMAG-
ined that other families were like the *Ozzie and Harriet* or the *Leave it to
Beaver* families. Only mine was different. My dreams and prayers were
for that kind of family. I escaped into books when I could get them, and
music—especially music. My dad had played in a country and western
band when I was very young, so music was always in our home. I guess
that's where I get my love of music. At a very young age, I was a fan
of Rock 'n' Roll, American Bandstand and Elvis. As a young teenager,
I loved the Beach Boys, the Beatles, and Rolling Stones; there weren't
many popular singers or groups that I didn't love. I also loved the classics
and developed an appreciation for some country music.

My music teacher in junior high school introduced me to Beethoven,
Bach, and Chopin. She also taught me about Gershwin and Rogers &
Hammerstein. A couple of my friends and I would spend our lunch time
in her classroom listening to her records. She would tell us more about
the composers than we had time for in our regular classes. Music was
my constant companion. When I was eleven, I bought a transistor radio
and went to sleep with it playing under my pillow every night. One of
my most treasured gifts was a little record player. Just about any money
I received went towards 45 rpm records for it. I truly believed that my
life would one day be like the words I heard on these songs I loved, full
of love and happiness.

Air conditioning was a luxury in the fifties and sixties; most homes did not have it. My family bought our first air conditioner when I was thirteen. My dad was a Rapid Transit bus driver, now called Metro. Earlier that year, the city purchased air-conditioned buses. Because of driving in the air-conditioned bus during the day and sleeping without it at night, he continued to get sick. Finally, he decided we needed it at home. Not everyone had a telephone or two cars or washers and dryers. We usually didn't lock our doors and never had our house burglarized. It's hard for me to recall the way things were back then. To young people today, it must sound almost like a made-up place compared to the way things are in their world.

As I said, my family was what, today, would be called dysfunctional. My dad had passed up several opportunities in his younger years. He was offered part ownership of a very large farm where he worked when I was a baby. All he had to do was stay there and work the farm for a certain number of years. He turned it down; I guess he was a restless young man. I was told by family members that my dad had been offered an opportunity when he was young from someone in the music industry. The guy had seen a raw talent in him and wanted to help him develop it. He turned it down. He played on live radio in a band during the early fifties when Elvis Presley was beginning his career. In fact, he played in some of the same places, at different times; their paths never crossed that I know of. He could have made a success of it, he'd been told by those who knew about such things. But he became enslaved by his addiction at an early age.

His problem started at the age of fourteen. During the last few years of his life, my dad overcame his addiction and was even baptized into the church. He became a good Christian man. I admired the way he allowed God to change his life during those last ten years before he passed away. I still hold some painful memories of growing up in such an environment. I have wondered how our lives would have been altered if he had chosen a different path. Would it have been better or worse? I cannot say. The choices we make in our lives sometimes take us in directions that are unexpected and perhaps unprepared for, as I would learn in the coming years. Only God is wise enough to lead us down the path that is right for us, but He doesn't force us, He lets us make the choice to allow Him to guide us or to make our own way. I was glad that my dad chose God to lead him in his last years.

My mother had a job as far back as I can remember. She was a shy person who was abused and mistreated, but she loved my dad. She was not available most of the time for my siblings and me. She was just trying to survive the life she had chosen. Like I said before, it was a different time. It was innocent in many ways, but not favorable towards women. Dean's mother was in a similar situation, except she did not work. She did not drive either. We were quite a pair, Dean and me. We understood and related to one another in many ways. Neither of us wanted to do the things our parents had done. He was always so tender and respectful of me. I was a little more independent, some may call it stubborn Dean called it feisty, than either of our mothers had been. This has served me well in much of my adult life to become what one of my friend's calls a survivor. It also fed the anger that has been inside of me all these years.

Much of what I learned about being a wife, and especially a mother, I learned from my grandmother. She taught me to sew, how to clean, how to crochet, some cooking, and how to care for babies and children. I inherited her sewing machine when she died and have used it for more than a few years. It's the one she used to teach me to sew. Many of the things I learned from the example of my parents, I had to unlearn as an adult. As hard as it is for me to believe, my dad is the one who gave me a respect for God. He had been very religious as a child. My grandmother introduced me to God's word with the pictures in her big family Bible. She would read it every morning and every night before she went to sleep. It is a practice I have adopted in my own life.

As I said before, since I was the oldest of three children, the responsibility of caring for the younger two was mine. My other chores included ironing, cleaning, and sometimes cooking. We did not have a washer and dryer, so most of my Saturdays were spent at the Laundromat while my mother did the weekly grocery shopping. She worked all week and we shared the weekend work. It was our routine each week. There wasn't much time for friends or a social life besides I couldn't bring anyone home to discover the painful secrets a child keeps when there is substance abuse in her home.

Becky was the only friend whom I had allowed to come to my house until Dean. I learned at an early age that I enjoyed being alone. I loved to sit outside under a tree, reading, or in my room listening to my music. I really liked to read and tried to always have books from the school library. The books were my escape from the situation at home.

During the school year, Becky and I and two other friends would go to the new mall near my house. We shopped, but rarely bought anything. We giggled and tried on clothes. One time my mother and Becky's mother gave us money to purchase our own shoes for school. It was just after the Christmas break and we walked the entire mall trying on many, many shoes. Finally, we made our choice and bought matching shoes. We were so proud of this new responsibility entrusted to us by our mothers, but when we went home and presented our choice to them, they were both furious. We had chosen some cute suede sandals; not at all appropriate for the remaining winter months that were wet and cold. Of course, there was no way we were keeping them; they had to be exchanged for something a little more practical. Lesson learned.

It wasn't the only time Becky and I upset our mothers. One time we took the bus downtown to a parade. I had to take my little sister with us. Becky's dad worked in town and he located a place for us to watch the parade from. We decided to go into a Woolworth store after he left us, and we lost my sister; she was nine-years-old. Luckily, she remembered how to get back to where Becky's dad worked. We were grounded for quite a while. Yes, it was a different time for sure. These excursions were about a year and a half before I met Dean.

Becky and I loved to have sleepovers and stay up giggling half the night. I always wanted to go to her house because I could relax with no tension or embarrassing moments. Our first boyfriends were brothers. Neither of us could date, but at school we would talk with them and hold hands as we walked in the halls. We were only twelve. This was my life until a few months before my fourteenth birthday. It was a very different and simple time, getting ready to explode in ways I could never have predicted or imagined.

I guess this is where my story really begins.

3. Take My Heart

I WAS ALWAYS A FEARFUL AND TIMID YOUNG WOMAN UNTIL I MET *him*. It was early August1964, that's when *he* came into my life. My aunt Cathy was visiting us from Lubbock and she could drive. She was only four years older than me. Almost every evening, Cathy would borrow our grandmother's car and we would go driving. The night I first met him, we were just driving around the area near the schools, as teenagers did a lot back then (gas was less than 30 cents a gallon). In those days, most cars didn't have air-conditioning, so we had the windows rolled down. "I'm hungry, why don't we stop at Bailey's for some fries and coke before we go home?" Cathy asked. Bailey's was the nearest drive-in diner to our home; one of the places the high school kids gathered to hang out. I agreed, and we were on our way. About a block before Bailey's came into sight, we stopped at a red light where a nice aqua blue and white 1956 Chevy pulled up beside us. It was clean and shining in the early evening light.

At thirteen I knew my cars. I could recognize any make and model of car, name most parts under the hood and could tell you what kind of engine it had. There was a lot I didn't know, but I became fascinated with cars. My dad would have me help him when he worked on our car. I was what I would call today a "girly girl" so most people didn't believe that I could hold my own discussing cars with the guys. The guys would laugh at me if I asked questions. "We thought you knew everything about cars," they would tease. I guess it was a little unusual for young girls back then to care about such things. Though I'm not so knowledgeable now about the modern cars with their computerized components, I still love the classics.

As I turned to look at the Chevy, three high school guys from inside the car started waving, whistling, and trying to talk to us. I'm sure they thought I was looking at them, but it truly was the car. I was not so bold as to flirt with guys; especially high school guys. But I might have noticed them first if the car hadn't been so great. *He* was in the back seat. One of the guys from the front seat asked, "Hey, where you ladies going?" My not-so-shy aunt said, "To Bailey's."

When the light changed to green, we were hoping that they would follow us there and naturally, they did. It was the summer before I turned fourteen and I was about to be a freshman in high school. They parked next to us as we pulled into Baileys. I felt a little uncomfortable because he kept staring at me. I learned later that *he* had "claimed" me, to his buddies, when we were at the red light. The fact is that I had my eye on one of his friends with a baby face, a shy smile, blue eyes, and blonde hair, but I guess there was some unwritten rule among guys about "claiming" a girl when you meet them.

It was a hot summer night, but I hardly noticed the heat with all the laughing and attention from him. When they got out of the Chevy and walked over to our car, I saw how good looking he really was. He was tall, about six feet two inches and thin, but not too thin. He had wavy black hair and a curl that fell over one side of his forehead; his eyes weren't brown nor were they green, but both. I guess that would be hazel eyes. His smile was the most charming thing about his looks. Once I looked into his eyes, saw his beautiful mischievous smile, and heard him talk, I knew he was the one for me and not his blonde friend who was very shy like me. Wow! I was mesmerized by him. I felt like my heart was in my throat and though I didn't realize it at the time, I had lost it to him that night. He had me at "Hi there."

"Hi there, my name is Dean, what's yours?" he said.

I told him, "My friends call me B.J."

He was definitely not shy like his blond friend, who was quiet and smiled a lot. He said, "Well, I'm going to be a *special* friend, so I'll call you 'Red'." I was confused until he made a few comments about my red hair.

I said, "Actually my hair is brown."

He just smiled and said, "Well no, it's red and besides I like that name for you." I must admit that when the light was shining on it, my hair did have some red highlights, but I had never thought of myself as a red head.

As we talked, he said that he had had a birthday a couple of weeks before. "So" I asked him, "How old are you now?"

"I'm seventeen. How old are you?"

Without thinking about it I said, "Sixteen." What had I said and why? I knew why. I was afraid he would just leave if I told him the truth. I had been mistaken for an older age many times and he seemed to believe my lie. Then again, he didn't ask what school I went to or what grade I was in. He probably knew I was lying, so I expected them to back off and leave, but they stayed for about two hours. He was charming and witty; he kept me laughing the entire time and he hardly took his eyes off my face.

We sat in our car with the doors open, Dean sat in the front seat beside me. The other two guys, Jamie, the blond, and Ed, the driver and owner of the Chevy sat in the backseat. Ed was several inches shorter than the other guys. He was not shy like Jamie, but not as cool as Dean. He was a little funny, and he did own the car.

We all ordered Cokes (Cathy and I forgot about the fries) and one of the guys paid for them. The five of us spent a couple of hours just talking and laughing; mostly laughing. They made us laugh a lot, the way teenage boys do when they are trying to impress girls and girls do when they are nervous around cute guys. I was hardly aware of the other guys, though. Cathy finally said, "We have to go. We are supposed to be home with the car soon." I didn't want to leave, but Cathy was right.

Ed was telling Cathy and Jamie a story about something so Dean called me outside the car. "I want to see you again. I want to call you," he said.

I looked down and smiled, but I didn't know what to say. Was this okay? My heart told me that I couldn't let him leave with the possibility of not seeing him again.

Then he asked, "Can I have your phone number?"

My heart was beating so that I thought he could hear it. I gave him my grandmother's number since we didn't have a phone. Granny lived next door to us and she was always a safe harbor in my stormy life. I adored her. She allowed us to share her phone and I knew she wouldn't mind that I had given him her number.

Driving home, we giggled with excitement over our new friends. "Wow," Cathy said, "That guy, Dean, couldn't take his eyes off you."

"He is so cute," I giggled, "and his smile gave me chills. I've never felt that way before. Cathy, he asked for my phone number."

"Did you give it to him?

"Yes, well Granny's number. Do you think it's okay, I mean for him to call me?" I asked her. Cathy shrugged her shoulders and smiled. "We'll just have to wait and see what happens."

I gasped, "What if he doesn't call? Oh, Cathy, what if I never see him again?

"Girl, you really flipped for this guy, didn't you?"

She had been staying at our Granny's house and would not be here much longer, so I stayed there with her that night. We stayed awake late into the night talking about how cute and funny the guys were. All I could talk about was Dean. Cathy kind of liked one of the guys, but she was leaving in a few days and besides she had a guy back in Lubbock that she was interested in.

"I hope he calls you before I leave," she said.

I tried not to be too hopeful; surely, he knew I wasn't sixteen. But I really wanted him to call me. "I don't know what I'll do if he doesn't call, Cathy. I really want to see him again."

She smiled and said, "Don't give up."

I hoped to hear from him in the next few days, but no call came. Cathy and I decided that he had not believed my lie and would probably never call. I was so disappointed, and tried to stop thinking about him, but he came to my mind a lot. When I closed my eyes, I could see his smile. It made me feel like butterflies were in my stomach. I had truly given him my heart. I was flattered that this great older guy had even given me a second look. Guys were beginning to take notice of me and I'd had a couple of "boyfriends", but they seemed so young to me and it didn't last long. Usually it was the older guys that were looking, and I knew they were too old for me. This was different somehow. It didn't matter to me what his age was, I wanted to see him, again and again. He was about to be a high school senior and our freshman classes were still in the junior high school building. There was little chance of me seeing him again.

Soon Cathy left for home and I was missing her a lot. She had helped me get through the summer after my best friend, Becky, had moved out of state the week after school was out. I was feeling very lonely with them both gone, but I had to focus on preparing for school. It was only two weeks away.

4. Feisty Is As Feisty Does

I WAS ALWAYS NERVOUS ON THE FIRST DAY OF SCHOOL, BUT I ALSO was relieved to have those hours away from the stress at home. It was strange for Becky to not be at school on the first day back. I had a few friends there, but it wasn't the same as a best friend. Making friends was hard for me. Though I would rather be at school than home, I was feeling alone on that first day. I thought of him several times during the day and it made me sad. I couldn't seem to get him out of my mind. This feeling was like waiting on something that wasn't going to happen, and I didn't know how to deal with it.

It was always stressful for me to go home, not knowing who would be there and what the mood would be. If my parents were at home, things would be very tense and maybe even worse. Each day after school I had to go straight home to take care of my little brother and sister if my parents weren't there. They were in elementary school and would arrive at the house about thirty minutes after I got there.

Finally, that first day was over and I was standing outside the school waiting for my bus to arrive. We had to cross the two-lane street to board when it arrived; a group of us started across when I saw *it*. The most beautiful automobile I had ever seen, even today it is the most beautiful car made, in my opinion. It was a new 1964, bright red Chevy Impala and it was stopped next to my bus waiting for the students to cross in front of it. The Chevy was a hardtop with all the windows rolled down and had a bright white interior. As you would expect, there were red fuzzy dice hanging on the mirror. Most cars had a bench seat in the front instead of separate bucket seats, like the ones today; this one had the bench. I saw there were three high school guys in the front seat and three in the back, but as shy as I was, I didn't dare to look at them. Then I heard someone yell, "Hey, hey it's you. Hey, Red!"

It was him! I stopped in the street and turned towards the car. After all these years, I can still see him, sitting in the back seat between two other guys. My heart started beating wildly when I saw him climb over Jamie to get to the window. He was hanging out of the window with that confident smile. The Impala was beautiful, but it and the other guys disappeared when I saw him. Except for Jamie, I couldn't even tell you who the other guys in the car were. Everything around me began to move in slow motion. All I could see was his handsome face with his charming smile framed in the window of that beautiful red Chevy; I thought it must be what heaven is like.

You know in a movie the way everything around the object of affection just vanishes and this one person is all you see. Though it was only a few seconds, time seemed to be standing still and I couldn't breathe. My heart was melting, but I was also annoyed that he acted like I should be impressed by him, even though he had not called me as he said he would.

Did he think I would rush to the car and grab him? That's exactly what I wanted to do; I was *so* captivated by him. I had thought of him daily since the night we met. The only thing I could think of to say was, "I thought you were going to call me!" The words came out in my most sarcastic voice as I turned away and tossed my "red" hair; I kept walking, got directly on the bus and purposely found a seat by the window, on the side where the red Impala was stopped. My heart was pounding, my hands were damp and shaking, and my stomach was aching. What had I done; what had I said? I knew he must be thinking that I was such a kid.

He could see me through the open window where I was sitting, which is why I chose to sit there. The bus was still loading, and I could see him turning his entire body around in the car to find me on the bus. He was yelling something to me that I couldn't hear and I also didn't hear him telling his friends, "That redhead is feisty." He told me about that much later. Feisty was not my intent. It was just all I could think to say and keep my dignity. My heart was fluttering, and I felt like laughing and crying and throwing up all at once, but I could not turn away; his eyes held mine in a hypnotic state. I wasn't smiling, but just looking. I had never experienced a reaction to anyone like this before.

The bus was still loading and the other guys in the car were waving and yelling to get my attention, also. Didn't they know that he was all I could see? Several of the girls on the bus were asking, "Ooo, look, who are those guys? Who are they yelling at? BJ do you know them?" I couldn't speak; all I could do was shrug my shoulders. He stopped yelling and waving, but we did not take our eyes off one another until the bus drove away. Just before the bus started moving, I smiled at him and he just shook his head as he smiled back at me.

It was totally out of character for me to speak out so boldly to a boy! I can't imagine, as shy as I was, why those words came out of my mouth. Maybe I wanted to challenge him or maybe I was just a little annoyed. I had no time to think, I just reacted. He recognized me! He had even spoken to me and called me the sweet nickname he had chosen for me on the night we met! I knew that now there would be no doubt in his mind that I had lied about my age. I was really embarrassed that I had been caught in the lie.

Even if he had kept my number, I was sure he wouldn't call now since he had seen the school that I was leaving from. A sixteen-year-old could not be a student in this school. "He is probably laughing at me to his friends right now," I thought. My heart ached at the thought of it and that's when I realized that he really did have my heart; he really did have me from that first "hi there." It hurt to know I would probably never talk to him again. I could just imagine seeing him somewhere and him acting like we were strangers. Maybe the next time I wouldn't act so goofy. Hopefully there would be a next time; and very soon. At least he now knew which school I attended. If he had lost my number, he knew where to find me; if he wanted to. My mind was whirling with all these thoughts at once. I didn't talk to anyone on the ride home; my mind was so full of Dean.

I was walking from the bus stop to my house when Granny called to me from the front porch. "You have a phone call." she said. I thought it was my neighbor from next door. I sometimes would babysit for her. But it wasn't her. "He's called twice," Granny whispered with a smile, as I walked past her into the house. She knew all about him from Cathy and me talking. He must have gone straight home after I got on the bus and called me. I was amazed that he still had my phone number. My heart was beating so quickly, and I was almost afraid to speak into the phone. I took a deep breath. "So, you do still have my phone number." I quipped.

"Sixteen, huh?" he chided.

What could I do but confess my lie. "I thought I would never see you again anyway," I told him, "So it wouldn't matter what I told you."

"What else did you lie to me about?" He asked.

"That was the only thing. I thought you would just walk away if I told you my real age" I answered.

"So, you didn't want me to walk away, huh?"

I didn't answer him; I just smiled.

"Was everything you told me about you the truth?" I asked.

"Yes, it was, I have no reason to lie about my age. So how old are you?" he asked. When I told him thirteen, he whistled and said, "Oh no! Do you tell all the guys that lie or just me?"

"Well, I don't usually talk to guys the way we talked that night." I answered. "I'll be fourteen in a few weeks."

He kept saying that he couldn't believe that I was only thirteen. "I thought you probably gave me a fake phone number, but not a fake age" he said.

"Is that why you didn't call, you thought I lied about my number?" I answered.

"Okay, we're even," he laughed.

What we talked about has totally left my mind, but we were on the phone for more than an hour. I couldn't wait to write to Cathy and tell her how I had seen him again and that he had called. I had to write to Becky about him, too. I was sure that she would be so excited for me.

He didn't call the next day. I was so afraid I wouldn't hear from him again now that he knew I was only thirteen, but two days later he called. I know he was not sure if he should, but he continued to call me. Sometimes he and his friends would drive by my school when I was leaving and wave to me. They weren't always in the same car, so I would be surprised when I saw him. Then they began stopping at the school to talk as I waited for my bus, instead of just driving by. I became acquainted with his friends, also.

Suddenly I had a lot of friends; girls who wanted to meet his friends. He only talked with me, though. We would talk until the bus arrived and he would call me when I got home. Then one day he asked me where I lived. I was afraid to tell him, and I was afraid not to. The next day he came to my house. He wanted to pick me up at school, but I knew that was way over the line my parents would allow. After a couple of weeks, he would sometimes go straight to my house and be there when I got home. We would just sit outside under a tree and talk while he held my hand. He kept me laughing constantly. I would tell him to leave after about an hour, before my parents came home. He said, "I'm not afraid of your parents. In fact, I want to meet them." Though he surely knew things were not great, he didn't know how stressful my home life was.

He started calling almost every day, whether he came over or not. Once Dean was in my life, I would daydream about him whenever we were not on the phone or together. Though I had always enjoyed being alone, it was being with him that made me know that I never wanted to be alone again.

I was spending a lot of time at Granny's. My mom knew that I had been talking with a guy on the phone, but when she started asking questions, I was nervous. "BJ, tell me about this guy you are talking to."

"He's just a guy, Mom."

"What is his name, how old is he?"

"His name is Dean."

"BJ…how old is this Dean?"

I finally had to tell her. She couldn't believe that I was talking to a guy who was seventeen. I was very afraid when I learned that she told my dad. He said, "Don't even think about dating him. He is way too old for you. You aren't even old enough to date. I know what a boy his age is looking for and you will not be it."

"Daddy, we only talk on the phone" I lied. I didn't dare tell him that Dean had been coming to our house when he was gone. I learned at an early age to always be obedient to my dad and he hated to be lied to, but my attraction to Dean was much stronger than my fear of my dad.

It wasn't long before my dad found out that Dean and I were seeing one another and not just talking on the phone. He was not happy, but this was a new experience for him and I don't think he knew what to do. He told me that I couldn't see or talk to Dean again. But I knew I would disobey my dad for maybe the first time. He had his own problems with his alcohol and, like every issue in our family, it was just ignored.

5. Sea of Serenity

JUST OFF THE BELTWAY, AND VERY NEAR MY HOME, THERE IS A beautiful cemetery. A curved two-lane road leads to the driveway and the two separate gate entrances. Just as you turn onto the driveway, there is a curve that opens up a sea of colorful fresh and silk flowers that almost surrounds you. As you continue around the curve, the sea grows wider and even lovelier. The drive winds around a bend on the southwest side of the grounds where there is a pond with a fountain in the center. There are ducks and swans that live there. It has always made my heart beat a little faster when I see this beautiful sight; not just the view, but the humble feeling it inspires. Just driving through the winding roads, you feel a kind of reverence.

There is a plethora of huge old live oak trees with gray Spanish moss hanging from their low reaching branches. They seem to be bending down to protect the occupants who are resting there. They spread their boughs over the sacred head stones and markers like a loving mother's arms reaching to protect her child. A breeze sings a soft lullaby as quietness settles in around the graves. Its beauty can only be surpassed by the serenity it offers.

In the center of this cemetery, there is a small antique chapel that is now a mausoleum. It dates back to another century. It has a kind of gothic appearance, as many eighteenth and nineteenth century churches did. Older grave markers and head stones are scattered out on both sides

26

and behind the small chapel; many of them are more than a hundred years old. A large funeral home and chapel had been built several years ago, just off one of the entrances from the main road. In recent years, it was torn down and a new, larger, more modern facility was constructed on the opposite side, away from the pond. I have watched the changes here throughout the years like an old silent film moving ever so slowly before my eyes.

Back when we were dating, the guys thought it was funny to try and scare their dates by telling a "true" ghost story while driving by this cemetery at night. The headlights would shine on the headstones, projecting an eerie sight. In those days, the meandering road that runs next to the south side of the cemetery was covered with gravel, and it was dark. There was barely room for two cars to pass one another. Some Friday nights we would gather there on the road with friends where the only lights were the headlights of our cars and the moon. The guys would talk cars and racing. The girls would just talk and watch their guys.

The cemetery was located a few miles outside of town at that time. Land was purchased near the cemetery with plans to build a new airport to ease the traffic of the William P. Hobby airport located on the south side of town. We had heard that the new airport would open in 1966. As most large enterprises do, it went over budget and took longer than planned. It finally opened on June 8, 1969 and was originally named *Jetero Intercontinental Airport*, and then more construction was done, and the name was changed to *Houston International Airport*. Eventually the airport had to be increased in size to accommodate the growing city and compete with Dallas/Fort Worth International Airport and the name was changed again to George Bush Intercontinental Airport after our former president who now lives in Houston.

The city had grown and spread out into the area where the cemetery was located, bringing the noise and traffic with it. The gravel road next to it was paved and houses built nearby. It seems that the highway that runs on the east side of the cemetery has continued to be enlarged every few years to accommodate the growing community with thousands of cars streaming through each day. It was the same highway that Dean and I always traveled to get to the creek with our friends for cookouts and swimming.

Even with the traffic and noise of the highway, this cemetery is a peaceful sanctuary. Any time of day and any day of the week, there are people visiting the graves of their loved one. Many times when I go, I see an older man or woman bringing flowers to a loved one; possibly a spouse. I can imagine they have been doing this for many years; it is a part of their Sunday afternoon routine. I see young parents with their small children walking hand in hand, and multiple generations of family sitting by a grave. Maybe they are telling the children about grandparents. An older couple comes to bring flowers and put fertilizer on the grass where her parents' graves are located. One word that describes what I see there is respect; respect for the ones who have passed over, and for their loved ones who visit there. It is a blessing for those who visit to have a private place to reflect on one they miss so desperately.

While visiting there several years ago, I jotted down these words that came to mind as I watched people come and go.

Visiting the Silent Land

Live Oak trees and green grass
Back drop and setting of this view
The grass is littered with flowers
Colors are more than a few
Ducks swim on a small pond
There's a fountain in its midst
The people come day by day
To remember loved ones missed.
Each one has a story
Each one an ache in their heart
Where there is a black hole
Since their loved one did depart.
Sometimes they add to the flowers
Sometimes only tears they bring
All have one common purpose
Each to their memories they cling.
O, how long have I come here
Trying to heal my heart?
Who can answer my plea?
Will God one day impart?

6. Crossing Paths to Love — 1964

EVEN IN A LARGE CITY THE SIZE OF HOUSTON, DEAN AND I DIS-
covered that our paths had crossed numerous times throughout our lives,
even though we never met. We had gone to the same elementary school
at the same time. I had attended there from kindergarten through the
sixth grade and Dean had only attended for his second and third grade
years. I must have been in kindergarten when he was there. Since he was
older, of course we didn't meet.

One evening in late October, Dean and I took my little sister to that
same school for a Fall Festival and saw our third-grade teacher, Mrs.
Elliot. We didn't know that she had taught both of us in third grade
until she called us both by name. She even remembered things about
each of us when we had been in her class. We were surprised that she
remembered us, even our names. As young children in her class, we both
thought she was very old, but she was still teaching and had a very good
memory. She had a strength and lovely manner about her that you see in
people who are kind to others; it comes from the inside. She was the person who made me fall in love with books and with reading. She always
read to the class, one chapter each day, after lunch, until the end of the
book. It was the highlight of my school day. I didn't remember anyone
reading a book to me before, though they may have.

During my growing up years, our family had driven by the house
where Dean and his family lived, every time we drove my dad to work.

The public pool I went to in the summer months was only one block from this same house where he lived.

When his family moved a few miles from there, the new location was two houses away from my best friend, Becky. They went to the same elementary school and all three of us went to the same junior high school, but years apart. As best friends, I stayed overnight at her house at least two or three times each month for two years before she moved away. We had another friend, Belinda, who lived a couple of blocks away. Becky and I would walk to Belinda's house and we would all go walking in the neighborhood. We would even go to the neighbor's house, which was between hers and Dean's, to visit another friend. Dean was a neighbor to Becky all that time, but he and I never met. Only God knew that the love of my life was so near to me throughout our childhood. I met him the same summer Becky moved away. When I wrote her about him, she was very surprised. She wrote me back and said knew who he was but did not like him at all. She said she thought he was in a gang or something and that he had fights all the time. She tried to tell me to stay away from him, but I knew that wasn't going to happen.

I learned that he was the oldest child in his family, as I was. Dean had two brothers, one who was older than me, and the other was my age. I went to school with them both, but I didn't know them. I was amazed at the similarities between our families and the parallel of our lives up to this point.

I always chose friends who were extroverts and they would draw me into a relationship. I was a shy person and always wanted to be in the background, watching rather than initiating activities or friendships. Once someone gained my trust, I wasn't so shy with them. Though they were not alike in other ways, Becky and Dean both had that outgoing personality; anything but shy. I think my relationship with both of them was for a lifetime.

A Date?

My parents surprised me by having a phone installed for my fourteenth birthday, since I was using Granny's phone so much. Now Dean and I could talk even more than before, and we did. Dean asked me to a movie the Saturday two days before my birthday. My dad was not happy about me dating him, but he said that if my mother would drive me there and pick me up that I could go. I guess he thought that arrangement would be embarrassing for me, which it was, or Dean would be put off by it. But Dean didn't seem to mind. In fact, he said, "I understand, they don't know me. You are only fourteen. After they get to know me, they'll trust me." He was right; my parents eventually grew to love him. After that, I guess it was too much trouble for my parents to drive me to my dates, so he was allowed to pick me up at home in his car.

I don't remember much about the movie we saw that day, but I was very aware of him sitting next to me. I had never been that close for that long to a guy I was attracted to. I was so afraid Dean would know that and really think I was a baby. I just wanted him to think of me as a girl he would date. My heart was racing when he reached over and held my hand. He was so gentle with me. After the movie, he waited outside with me until my mother came to get me. He spoke to my mother and thanked her for letting me see the movie with him. You might think he was one of those charmers that act one way with adults and a total jerk when they weren't around, but he wasn't that way at all. He was confident and had a great sense of humor. He kept me laughing, but as I came to know him better I could see how sincere he was with everyone. What you saw is what he truly was.

7. Who is This Guy?

I was so excited when Dean asked me out for the first real date the weekend after my birthday, less than two months after we met. I had told him that I couldn't date until I was fourteen and he waited for me. From that point on, we went out at least once each week. Looking back, I'm sure my parents were thinking when I started dating at fourteen it would be with someone closer to my age; someone who didn't drive.

On our first date, we went to the Prince's drive-in where some of his friends liked to hang out, and a few of mine did, too. Dean always opened the driver side door for me to get in and sit close to him. I felt so special sitting next to him as our friends could see us. I've heard it said that "a nervous silence loosens the tongue" and I was very nervous. When I realized I was talking a lot, I could feel my face redden with embarrassment. He was just smiling at me. "Why don't you talk for a while," I said to him and he laughed out loud.

"I haven't heard you talk so much before; I like it." He smiled. We just sat in his car and talked for a long time. There were so many things I wanted to know about him and I guess he wanted to know about me also. After some time, we just drove around here and there for a while, just talking and getting to know one another better. It was a wonderful evening; my first real date. We drove down Jamie's street, which was the same street where Becky had lived. Dean stopped next to Jamie's house for a while. His friend Bud and some other guys were there. Jamie said they had been "shooting hoops." Some of them I had met before when he stopped to see me after school; the others he introduced me to. We then drove a couple of blocks and he stopped outside another house and said, "Come with me."

It was two houses from Becky's old house. I asked him, "What are you doing? Who lives here?" Maybe my instincts were wrong about him; I felt a little anxious.

"Just come with me," he smiled. He took my hand and we went inside where I met his parents. They were not expecting me, but they stopped watching television to be introduced. Dean and I had only met a short time ago and he was eager to introduce me to his parents! My head was spinning, and my heart was full of love for him already. He was surprised later when I told him about being friends with Becky and staying there so much. "How could we never have met or even seen one another?" I asked him.

"I probably didn't notice you because you were with her," he said. "She's your best friend? But she is just a kid!" I didn't remind him that she and I were the same age.

His grandmother and aunt lived near his family, just as mine lived near me. It wasn't long until I had met them all. He loved his family. We both had several family members that lived in the Houston area.

When he took me home, he walked me to the door. He hugged me and held me close to him for a couple of minutes. Then he kissed me once on my lips so softly. I was sure he could hear my heart beating in my chest. I could hardly sleep that night; I just wanted to remember each minute with him.

More Dating

The first week in November, the cool weather had arrived; we went out again to a movie. As I sat next to him, the movie was not what I was thinking about. That night when he took me home, Dean kissed me, really kissed me, for the first time. As young as I was, I had been kissed a few times by my first boyfriend. But this was my first real kiss. I knew I wanted those kisses for the rest of my life. There was nothing official between us, yet. We had only known one another for three months at that time.

One night, after we had been dating for several weeks, Dean and Jamie came to pick me up to go out to a drive-in movie. They were waiting for me to finish my hair and then we were going to pick up Jamie's date on the way. Just before we left, we saw a guy walking up the driveway to my front door. It was a guy I knew from school. He was a year older than me and was always talking to me. I knew he liked me. I was polite to him, but I wasn't interested in him and didn't know how to tell him. When he got close to the front porch, Dean asked, "Who is this guy?"

"He's just a guy I know from school," I answered.

"Do you want us to leave?" He asked.

"No, he's just a friend," I said.

"I don't think he's walking to your house because he wants to be your friend," Dean answered. He didn't say another word, but opened the door, went out and shut the door behind him. I looked at Jamie and he just shrugged his shoulders and smiled. I couldn't hear what he said, but I saw Dean talking as he walked the guy to the driveway with his arm on his shoulder. The guy left and never talked to me again. He did not have a car and had walked five miles to see me.

"Dean, what did you say to him? You were nice, right?" I asked him.

He said, "Sure, I was nice. I just told him that you were my girl and he didn't need to come to your house again."

35

I looked at Jamie again and he was still smiling, almost laughing. I felt bad for the guy and a little embarrassed but was thrilled that Dean had told him that I was *his* girl. It was the first time he had said it. That was the night he asked me to wear his senior ring. I treasured it as I proudly wore it around my neck on a gold chain.

Loyal Friend?

Dean's friend Ed, who owned the 1956 Chevy that he, Dean, and Jamie were in the night we met, would come with Dean to my house sometimes. They would play basketball in my driveway with my little brother. The way Ed looked at me always made me uncomfortable; he reminded me of Eddy Haskell from *Leave it to Beaver*. One night, Ed showed up at my house without Dean. He wanted me to come outside; he wanted to talk to me about Dean. I went out and asked him, "Why are you here. Where is Dean?"

He took hold of my hand. I pulled it away and he said, "Dean's at home, I guess. I just wanted you to give me a kiss. I just want one kiss and then I'll leave. I won't tell Dean." "You are Dean's friend!" I answered. Then I turned to go inside; he grabbed my arm and smiled.

He said, "If you don't kiss me, I'm going to get Dean and take him to a party tonight where there are a lot of pretty girls."

I pulled my arm away and ran inside the house. I went to my room crying. I was right about him, he was a jerk. The next day, Dean came over and said, "I didn't call last night because Ed and I were at Jamie's house playing basketball. Did you miss me?"

"Not really. Ed came to see me before you guys went to Jamie's," I answered.

"What! Why did he come to see you?" he asked.

I told him, "He just wanted a kiss, but he didn't get one. He threatened to take you to a party where there were a lot of pretty girls if I didn't kiss him."

Dean didn't say anything; he just squeezed my hand and left immediately. It was the only time I ever saw him look angry. I never saw Ed again. Dean never explained or spoke of him again and I never asked. He was very protective of me. He wouldn't let anyone treat me bad or even use crude language around me. That was fine with me. It just made me more determined to not give my heart away to anyone else.

After this incident, I wondered about what Becky had said about him being in a gang and fighting, so I asked him. He just laughed. He said, "Guys fight sometimes. It doesn't mean anything. I'm not in a gang, so no there have been no gang fights." He said there was no gang, just he and his friends from school, whom I had met. He said, "She probably thought that because my friends and I drive our cars around the neighborhood. Sometimes we get a little loud. You've met all my friends. There is no gang."

8. *Hiding A Broken Heart — 1965*

MY YOUNG TEENAGE YEARS WERE IN THE TURBULENT SIXTIES. Just weeks following my thirteenth birthday, President John Kennedy was assassinated. I remember how sad the country was and how I couldn't comprehend the impact of such an event on the world. Of course, I was aware of the racial problems in the country, but it wasn't touching me personally; the rioting was just on the television news. Surely it wouldn't have a big effect on us. I didn't pay much attention to the man who would become such an icon in American history, Dr. Martin Luther King, Jr. Though I didn't see it coming, as I look back I realize that I was living on the brink of the emotional eruption that was moving quickly across our nation.

Since my parents were gone most of the time, I was at home every day after school and all day during the summer taking care of my brother and sister. I wasn't allowed to leave the house until my mother came home from work, but Dean could call me just about any time. He could cheer me up or make me forget whatever was going on at home with his witty stories. Sometimes Jamie or one of their friends were with him and we would all talk. His sense of humor was only one of the reasons I loved being with him. Laughing wasn't a common thing in our home. No doubt about it, I was head over heels in love with Dean Whitlock. For Christmas, five months after we met, he gave me an ID bracelet with my name on one side and his on the other.

"I really care about you very much, Red, but I probably shouldn't. You are so young. Fourteen and seventeen, that's a big difference in our ages," he would say.

"It's only numbers. It doesn't mean anything." I told him. "I just want to be with you."

I was always fearful until I met Dean; he was my knight who took away my fear. My only fear was that he would see that I wasn't pretty enough, smart enough, or old enough for him to give me his heart as I had given him mine. I was so afraid he would let his mind overrule his heart. A couple of months later, that was exactly what he did. He came to my house after I came home from school, just as he had many times, but he was acting different. "I just can't do it, Red" he told me, "I feel guilty all the time because you are so young. We are getting too serious. I think you should see other guys."

"I don't want to see other guys!" I told him.

He argued, "If you don't date other guys you can't be sure about how you feel about me."

"I know how I feel about you! I don't want to date anyone else!" I answered. "Is that what you really mean? Do you really want me to date other guys or do you want to date other girls?" I asked him.

He didn't answer; he just looked in my eyes and shook his head. I returned his ring and he left. Watching him drive away was tortuous. Would I ever see him again? I was devastated; I couldn't stop crying.

After Dean broke up with me and took his ring back, I had so much pain in my heart. I couldn't eat or sleep. I had met Jamie's little sister at school and we became friends. She told me that Dean had gone out with Bud's girlfriend's sister. It hurt me so much to think of him with another girl. Two or three guys asked me out when they learned Dean and I were not together, but I wasn't interested in them. He was all I wanted.

One guy I had known since we were young kids asked me to go with him to get something to drink. He knew I was hurting. He picked me up on his motorcycle, which he thought would cheer me up. He knew I love riding. Before we reached Bailey's, I was done with the evening. "Do you want to talk about it or go home," my friend asked. I went home.

It didn't take long for the word to get out that I wasn't interested in dating anyone. Other guys meant nothing to me and Dean meant everything. I tried to pretend that I was fine. My close friends at school knew how my heart was breaking. They tried to cheer me up, but it was useless. I just sat through my classes writing Dean's name on my notebook over and over. Since my parents were not home much they didn't know how I was hurting. I was accustomed to hiding my feelings. I had learned to be a pretty good actress as children of alcoholics do. But every night in my room I would slide my transistor radio under my pillow, listen to my music, and cry myself to sleep. That's the first time I understood the term *broken heart*. It felt like my heart was shattered inside my chest. I was sure it would just stop beating soon.

Every day I watched for his car everywhere I went. One day about three weeks after we had been apart, I saw it. Dean was driving by my school one afternoon just as I was coming out to go home. He was looking at me, but when he saw me look up at him, he turned his head, sped up, and was gone. My heart ached at the sight of him. The first thought I had was that it was just a coincidence, but the next day I saw him again, and the day after that. He pretended not to see me, but I knew he had.

Then I learned from Jamie's sister that he had not dated anymore. It was the first spark of hope I had. I devised a plan to get his attention and see what he was up to by driving by the school. I was sure he cared about me, maybe even loved me. I knew I loved him. I wanted him back, so I took a chance the next day. I borrowed a letter jacket from my friend "Robert" who was on the football team. I'd told him I was cold and asked for his jacket. His name was stitched across the back. I put it on as he and I stood talking in front of the school, where I had seen Dean drive by. Maybe it was a little obvious, but what did I have to lose. We were standing close to the street and when I saw Dean's car coming down the road. I turned my back to the road and started talking to Robert. The jacket was a really big deal since the girls usually wore a guy's jacket if they were going "steady." I didn't know if he even saw me, so as I rode the bus home, I was anxious. Maybe I had done the wrong thing. What was I thinking?

To my amazement and joy, it worked. He turned into my driveway as I got off the bus in front of my house. I tried to play it cool, even though my heart was beating so hard, as it always did whenever he was near me. I wanted to run into his arms when he stepped out of his car, but I knew I had to see what he had to say. He just smiled that charming smile that melted my heart and said, "Hey Red."

"Hi, Dean, what's going on?"

"I was just driving, and I thought I'd stop and say hi," he answered. "So, how are you doing?"

"I'm fine," I answered. I knew he didn't just happen to be in my neighborhood, but I wasn't sure what to say next.

"Can we sit by the tree?" he asked.

"Sure" I answered. We walked over to the tree and we sat down on the cool grass. It had become "our tree" when we were together, where we could talk without my brother and sister around.

We sat there making small talk for a few minutes, about school and friends, nothing important. I wanted to scream at him; I wanted to grab him; I wanted to punch him. But after a few minutes of small talk, I calmly asked him, "Dean, why are you here?"

Then he answered, "I was driving by the school today and saw you talking to some guy. Was that his jacket you were wearing?"

"His name is Robert and yes it was his jacket," I answered.

"Are you two together, now?" he wanted to know.

"No, we aren't together, we're friends. When I told him I was cold he gave me his jacket," I answered.

41

Dean reached for my hand and I didn't pull away. He looked down at our fingers clasped together, "I have missed you, Red" he said quietly. Then he looked in my eyes and said, "Baby, I want us to be back together again?" He had never called me "Baby" before.

I couldn't stop the tears in my eyes when I said, "I've missed you too." He put his arms around me and held me for a long time. We talked for a little while longer and then he placed his senior ring on my finger. "Is that okay?" he asked. When I answered yes, he kissed me.

I smiled and asked him, "Hey, did you call me a baby, because of my age?"

"No, I was calling you *my Baby*; there's a difference," he answered. During our first year, he broke up with me twice more; he still had a problem with my age. The first time was the longest time we were apart. It had been the longest and most difficult weeks in my life. The other times it lasted only a couple of weeks but seemed much longer and it hurt. Neither of us dated anyone else. I never kissed or dated another guy after I met him. As I said before, there was no one I wanted except Dean.

Yes, we did have a disagreement from time to time and he would stay away for a few days. The arguments were always about the same thing. Our feelings were so strong for one another. I wanted to wait, and he didn't. It was a problem. "Baby, I love you so much that I think I'll go crazy" he would say.

"I love you too, Dean, but it's not right. Be patient with me please," was my usual answer. I guess my fear and common sense won out over his raging hormones. My hormones were raging, also, but I was afraid and had been taught that sex before marriage was wrong. So, we made a promise to one another to only date when we were with other couples and the other times we went to very public places. We would go to the drag races and movies or just hang out at my house or a friend's house. These were *safe* places where we could spend time together with other people around. The only place we were alone is sitting under "our" tree in my back yard. Those times were great for talking and a little hugging and a kiss or two.

Today's girls would laugh at the morals I had back then. It wasn't a religious thing, I didn't know much about such things; it was a right and wrong issue mixed with a lot of fear. But it was in the early sixties before the sexual revolution became so widespread across America. I had been taught that it was wrong, and I was a *rule follower* at heart. Abstinence was not only acceptable; it was practiced by many girls.

It wasn't long before it was evident that the world as we knew it was changing. I heard stories about a group they called "hippies" living in California. The drugs, "free love", and other things that were rumored about them were foreign to me. The kids at school that were thought to use drugs were whispered about and they stayed to themselves away from most of the students.

I was a typical teenager who liked the Beatles (Ringo was my favorite because he was the drummer; most of my friends were crazy about Paul). Sonny and Cher seemed like the perfect couple to me and I tried to imitate Cher's long straight hairstyle. My mother hated it. The bangs were easy to emulate, but I couldn't get my hair to lie straight and smooth like hers. Ironing it was my only option.

Because of Dean, my life was good, and I was happy for the first time that I could remember. It was the first time I remember feeling loved. I thought I could handle anything if we were together. He was everything to me. He was my reason for breathing and for my heart to keep beating. I'm not sure if he knew how much I loved him. When we were together, I couldn't see or hear anyone else. Even watching a movie, his hand holding mine was still all I could focus on. For the most part, I can't remember who was with us when we were together, but my recollection of him is clear in my mind. It didn't matter to me where we went or who we were with as long as we were together.

9. Love, Cars, And Rock 'n Roll — 1965-1966

OUR WHOLE LIVES WERE AHEAD OF US AND WE WERE ENJOYING IT. These feelings were exciting and new for both of us. We spent hours on the phone or sitting under the tree in my yard talking about our dreams and plans. I started calling him "Deanie Poo," just to hear him protest, but I think he secretly liked that I teased him the way he teased me. We were always holding hands. Just the touch of his hand was electric to me. When the weather was cold we cuddled while sitting on the hood of his car; rainy weather found us sitting inside his car in my driveway laughing and talking for hours or just holding one another quietly while listening to the radio. I felt so safe and peaceful with him. The world was far away from our thoughts or at least from my thoughts. All I cared about or could see was Dean.

Dean loved cars and he liked that I could understand what he was talking about when he talked about cars. He would tell his friends, "My girl knows her cars." He had the greatest 1958 Ford Fairlane. It was a black hardtop with a gold stripe along the sides. I felt like a princess sitting close to him in that car, not because of the car, but because of him.

Dean was handsome; confident and strong in many ways. At five feet two inches and about 110 pounds, I felt small and protected next to his six feet, two inches. He wore jeans and striped button up shirts, always starched and ironed perfectly. His smile could melt an iceberg. In my eyes, he was the most handsome guy I had ever seen. He was smart, funny, compassionate, sweet, and my knight in shining armor.

Several months after we met, Dean left his parent's home. He and his dad were not getting along. He moved into his aunt's house. His grandmother, his cousin, and her little girl lived there also. They lived only a few blocks from his parents, in the same neighborhood. He decided to drop out of high school in his senior year and get his GED. He needed to get a job to support himself. Then he went to work for his uncle, who was a construction contractor, building new houses. Sometimes he would take me with him to his aunt's house and I would visit with his grandmother while he changed clothes upstairs. She was such a sweet person and she would show me pictures of him and tell me about him when he was a child. She said he was born in Little Rock, Arkansas, and she gave me a picture of him at the age of about ten or eleven. She loved Dean as any grandmother loves her grandchild and I enjoyed listening to her talk about their family. It was as if Dean and I had always known each other; we understood one another, which only encouraged our strong feelings. I knew that we were created to be together.

After a few months, Dean, Jamie, and Bud moved into an apartment together. We promised one another and promised my parents, that I would never go to his apartment unless there were friends with us. Sometimes we would take his youngest brother along with us to go swimming in the pool. Most of the time we were at my house, Prince's Drive-in, or at the homes of friends, but we did hang out at the apartment a few times with several of our friends. We ate pizza, or a couple of times I cooked for them, and we listened to records; the *Animals, Beatles, or The Rolling Stones;* an old Platters album was one of our favorites. We both loved music of all types. It was innocent fun just laughing, eating, and talking the way kids do. We were really all kids trying to be grown-ups in a changing world, but we still wanted to be young.

Before the end of the summer, one year after we met, we could no longer control our emotions. Though we tried to keep the promise we had made to my parents and one another, it was eventually broken. We spent so much time together that it was inevitable. We had started talking about how things would be and what we would do after we were married. There was no proposal, it was just a given. We both knew that getting married was in our future. Waiting just didn't seem important to me now; we were in love. I could wait no longer to truly belong to him.

Independence

I had a friend who worked at a small mom and pop ice cream & hamburger shop close to my school. He talked to his boss about hiring me and she agreed. I loved having a little money of my own. I worked during the summer and after school. Granny had offered to watch my brother and sister. If he got off work early enough, he would be waiting outside the school to take me home or to work.

The more independent I became, the more I made my own rules. I had always been one of those kids who did what I was supposed to do; I really was a rule follower. The teachers loved me, and my parents trusted me more than they should have. I must confess that many of the things I did were my idea, but Dean didn't discourage me much. There isn't much that I wouldn't do if he had asked me. He was the only good in my world. My World History class was the last class of my day and the room had two doors. One of the doors was next to the side door of the school that went outside. It was on the side of the building facing towards my job a block away. There were some days when I would leave out of the back door after the roll was called and meet him at my job for a Coke and talking until time for me to go to work. It's no wonder I couldn't keep up with all the world happenings, I wasn't in class enough to hear about them. I don't know how I passed that class with a C.

Occasionally when we had not been able to see one another for a couple of days, Dean would come to my house, late after my parents were asleep. Understand that their substance abuse made things difficult for me and was very distracting for my parents during this time. I would sneak out and we would go to Bailey's or just sit in my driveway and talk for a long time. We planned our future together sitting in his car. "I want children," he said. "I want you to have my children."

"And how many children will we have?" I asked.

"At least two, a girl and a boy. Is that o.k. with you? And I'll build a house for us to live in." He smiled.

There were times when I would get back inside the house and into bed just before the alarm went off for my parents to get up for work. They got up very early. Many times, he would call me after my parents were asleep; the phone was downstairs and I would sit on the floor next to it and grab it before the first ring finished. We would talk and laugh way into the night. In the summer, it wasn't hard, but I'm not sure how I kept my grades up during the school year with so little sleep.

My mother car pooled with a co-worker and one day when she left her car in the driveway, I took her keys and drove to pick up Dean and take him to get his paycheck and back to his aunt's house. I was just barely fifteen and did not have a drivers' license. I was afraid even though I was gone for only an hour. My mother did not know about that incident until about twenty years later when I confessed to her. She was shocked. I am really surprised myself when I look back. It wasn't like me at all, but love can make you do things you never thought you would do.

We just couldn't get enough of being together. I can almost hear his voice even now, "I love you, Red," or "BJ let's ask Jamie if he wants to get a date and go see a movie tonight," he would say. I had always hated my name, but when he said it or called me one of his sweet names it was beautiful. Sometimes he would call me "Baby Cakes" when we were alone or later in the letters he wrote to me. He made me feel like the world was ours when I was with him. I don't think either of us had ever had a positive self-image before we met.

Because of him, I began to dream of things I could do, things that we could do together. I had never dared to have dreams of doing anything. I didn't even think of going to college or having a career or any kind of future. It had never occurred to me that I could even make plans for my future. I had lived day to day, not knowing what would be happening in my life tomorrow; survival was my goal. He gave me self-confidence to think about my future. It's no wonder I fell so completely for him. He said I made him feel like he was loved completely; and he was. We had a need for one another. I finally felt like I mattered to someone.

10. Beginning of Fear

Dean had his eighteenth birthday in the summer of 1965. He got a job in the factory, where my mother worked. In October, I turned fifteen and life was good. On a cool day, in the middle of November, he came to my house unexpectedly; he said he wanted to talk to me about something. He was leaning against the front of his car with his arms around me. I wasn't expecting him to come to see me until the evening. I was surprised, but thrilled, that he was there. As he held me in his arms, he gave me his news. "I'm going to tell you something that may upset you; just remember that I love you," he said.

It frightened me. It had been a long time since he broke up with me. Had he found another girl? Could I be wrong about us? Were we breaking up again? I certainly wasn't prepared for what he told me next. "I'm about to be drafted into the Army, so today I went to the recruiter and enlisted; I will be leaving before Christmas," he said. At first, I thought he was joking since he was always teasing me. He just wanted to get a rise out of me. I smiled. He didn't. I knew he was serious.

"No, you can't; not yet! Just wait," I cried. I didn't know about Vietnam or that we had recently sent troops there to fight. I just didn't want him to leave me. What if he found another girl he loved more than me? I was young; my world consisted of Dean, keeping peace at home and school. I didn't care about the outside world and I didn't think it could touch us. I knew there was a chance he would be drafted one day, but I didn't pay attention to the news about some faraway place. I had more important interests; I was in love.

"How could you do this without telling me? How can you leave me?" I cried. I was upset, but not as much as I was about to be, as he talked about war.

"I knew you would try to talk me out of it, Red, but it is my duty to serve my country," he answered. "I thought the sooner I went in, the sooner I would get out. By then you will be out of school and we can be married. Wait for me and write to me? We'll see one another whenever I come home on leave," he said.

I couldn't even speak with the tears in my eyes and the ache in my heart.

"The only thing that bothers me is I'm afraid that you will find someone else while I'm gone," he said.

I said to him, "Dean, I have had opportunities to go out with other guys. I'm not interested in them. You are all I have ever wanted. I'm not going to find someone else, trust me." He just held me as I wept. He had tears in his eyes too, but he had more control than me. I believed him, but I was terrified.

Dean was an honorable and honest guy. He felt a strong responsibility to defend and fight for his country. The South Vietnamese people needed help. He told me some about what was happening there. He wanted to help; it was just like him to care about people he didn't even know. He was determined to be a soldier and not an ordinary soldier, but a paratrooper. The chill I felt that day was more than the northern breeze that had blown in that afternoon. I wanted to hold on to him and never let him go.

His dad had fought in World War II and I think he also wanted to prove to his dad that he was a man. We had grown up watching World War II movies and it seemed to glorify war somewhat. Vietnam, we were to learn, was not remotely like his dad's war.

50

We spent almost every day together from that day until he left two weeks before Christmas. For some reason, all the new recruits that had gone to Fort Polk that week were given a pass to go home for ten days before Christmas. During those ten days together, Dean and I became even closer to one another. We spent as much time together as we possibly could. He was back for ten days and then gone again. It was so hard to let him go for the second time. We wrote to one another and it made me so happy that he would declare his love for me in his letters. I could not love him more.

Connected Through Music

We had always been connected through the music we both loved, and Dean started learning to play the guitar before he enlisted. He loved all kinds of music, including country music. Our first movie together, when my mother had taken me to meet him, was *The Hank Williams Story*. He would practice playing the guitar as we sat under our tree and he would sing *Together Again*. Then he would smile and say, "Remember when we were *together again*?" He was referring to our first break up.

"Yes, I do," I'd say. He vowed to learn to play well enough to sing it to me *for real* when he returned from Basic Training.

He called me one evening after about six weeks to say he had a weekend pass if he could get a ride home. I missed him so much and begged my mother to take me to get him. She finally agreed. We left very early on Saturday morning for Fort Polk, Louisiana, which was a three-and-a-half-hour drive. It seemed like it took forever to get there. I couldn't wait to see him. Finally, there he was walking towards our car. The Army had cut off his wavy hair, but he looked great to me. He brought me some pictures of him and his buddies. One of them he had signed "Deanie Poo" which made me smile. It was hard to just hold hands as we rode in the front seat with my mother, though we did share a small kiss or two or maybe three. It seemed like we had been apart for months or years instead of a few weeks.

It was a weekend of mixed feelings. We were together the entire day on Saturday, late into the night and on Sunday until he had to leave. He had already learned to play the guitar well enough to play and sing *Together Again* to me. He knew every word. I felt very sad as he sang it to me a few times that evening because I knew there would be many more times we would be separated now. *Together again. My tears have stopped falling… And nothing else matters, We're together again.*

It seemed that our relationship had become so much stronger. That night we were sitting on the grass outside my house and Dean had just finished singing, *"I'm So Lonesome I Could Cry"* as he played his guitar. That is when he confessed to me that didn't have a weekend pass. He had gone A.W.O.L. (absent without leave) because he missed me and couldn't wait any longer to see me. We held each other as I cried. Dean even shed a few tears. I had never seen him cry, it broke my heart. That explained why he was staying with my cousin Tessa and her husband who had moved next door to us. He did not want to go home to see his parents while he was here. That would not have gone well, I'm sure.

What he had volunteered for was becoming as real to me as it had to him. I was beginning to understand some of what we would surely face. Our future together was so uncertain. We drove him back to camp the next day. It was hard to let him go again. Thankfully, he wasn't caught. Something had changed between us that weekend. It was more than just a physical connection; I knew that our souls were cemented together. We knew what one another was thinking; we could communicate without speaking. It seemed we were becoming one person in two bodies.

11. Together Again — 1966

A FEW WEEKS LATER, HE WAS HOME AGAIN. HE WOULD BE HOME for two weeks before going to Fort Gordon, Georgia for AIT (Advanced Individual Training) and then to Fort Benning, Georgia for Jump Training. Dean had a friend that he grew up with and gone to church where he and his mother worshiped. They were in Fort Polk together, also. He lived near us and we went out with him and his girlfriend a couple of times while they were both home. One night we went to a place where there was a band and we could dance. I had grown up dancing with all the music around me, but I was surprised that Dean could; we had never danced together. We only danced to the slow songs so that we could be in one another's arms.

Our emotions were overwhelming as we spent every minute possible together. I even skipped some days from school, without my parents knowing. I knew my parents were getting concerned about how much time we were spending together. The night before Dean left for Georgia, my dad confronted us about how serious we were. I guess we were not hiding our passion as well as we thought we were, but I'm sure he didn't know that our relationship had been intimate for a year already. Dean stood between my dad and me; he was afraid I may need to be protected. Then he said to my parents, "I'll be back in two months and we're getting married." My dad declared that we would not, but Dean would not back down. He told my dad, "I am telling you as respectfully as I can, Sir, that with or without your permission we will be married when I return. I'll be going to Vietnam soon after that." He was adamant. Finally, after some persuading by Dean and my tears, my dad said he would think about it.

When we were saying good night he said, "I didn't get a chance to talk to you before about not waiting until I'm discharged to get married. The way your dad was talking, I thought he was going to try and make us stop seeing one another and I couldn't let that happen. He can think about it or not, but we will be married when I return. I had already decided that if you agreed we wouldn't wait. I can't go over there with us not married."

"You really are serious," I smiled.

"Yes, I am." Dean said, "We can't wait. I am going to Vietnam. I want to know, while I'm there, that we belong to one another and that you're waiting for me. I want to take care of you."

"You know I will wait, whether we're married or not." I said. "Spending my life with you is all I want; I love you."

He said, "I thought we would have a fight on our hands with your parents, but whether they agree or not, we will be married."

I didn't know how he would make that happen, but I believed him and trusted him with all my heart. My emotions were all over the place; thrilled that we would be married soon, but so afraid of him going to war.

Though our parents were not in favor of it because we were so young, they finally gave in. I asked my mother, many years later, why they didn't stop us. She said that they talked about how I would feel about them if they had denied us that time together and he didn't make it back.

Before he left, Dean made it clear to my parents that if anyone gave me problems while he was gone, they would answer to him. My dad respected Dean and believed him. He knew Dean loved me and would take care of me. I am so thankful that our parents understood how we felt and gave us that time together. He would be in Georgia for two months and come back as a "Screaming Eagle" in the 101st Airborne

Division. I was so proud of him, but anxious at the same time. Vietnam was in our future, but when it was past us we could continue the life we had planned together. I held tightly to that thought.

It had been two years since that wonderful night at Baileys when we met. He was almost nineteen and I would be sixteen three months after the wedding. I was still in school and I still had my job on weekends, so I stayed busy. I wrote him every day about school and our friends. Jamie had been drafted into the Army and Bud enlisted in the Marines. Bud's fiancé, Mary, and I spent some time together going to movies and one weekend with Bud's parents on their boat as we waited for our guys. This "conflict" was growing so fast and affecting many people we knew. I was becoming more and more concerned.

My mom and I planned a small wedding. I bought an adorable white dress. It was sleeveless, had a straight skirt that was above my knees. It was covered with white lace. I asked my grandmother if we could get married in her house and of course, she agreed.

My entire family loved Dean. Three weeks before Dean would be home, my aunts gave us a wedding shower. I was so excited to see the things we would make our home with when he came back from Vietnam.

We decided to have the ceremony with only close family and friends in attendance. The minister of the church where his mother worshipped would officiate. I could hardly wait for the day to arrive. He returned home on Friday. In those days, you had to have blood tests and wait three days for the results before you could get a marriage license. Our doctor rushed the tests for us, so we got the results late Monday morning. We went downtown to the courthouse that same day, with both of our dads, to apply for the marriage license. On Tuesday morning, he picked me up and took me with him to pick up the wedding ring, but he would not let me see it until the wedding. I gave him back his high school ring that we had shared for almost two years. Everything was a go to have the ceremony that afternoon. It was really happening.

55

My dad took me to breakfast early that morning; just the two of us; which he had never done. He had stopped drinking several weeks before and stayed off it for several months. I think he was trying to say he loved me. He surprised me with a beautiful white corsage to wear on my pretty white lace dress. Dean wore his uniform and his high school ring I had returned to him. I felt beautiful and was so full of love for my handsome soldier.

My parents, Mr. & Mrs. Whitlock, our friends Jamie, Bud, and Mary, Granny, and just a few family members were there to witness our vows to one another. The wedding was simple but sweet. As the minister asked us, we each said, "I do." I was ecstatic when the minister pronounced us Mr. and Mrs. Alan Dean Whitlock and we shared our first kiss as husband and wife.

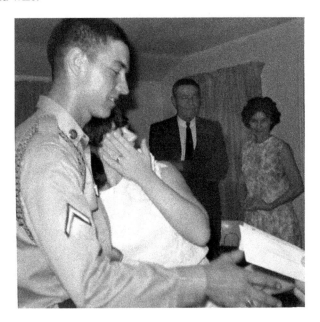

It was Tuesday, June 7, 1966. I guess I should have been a little afraid, but I had complete trust in him. A few pictures were taken with everyone smiling. There was no reception; there had not been time or money to plan one. Then Bud and Mary, who were planning to be married soon, drove us to Prince's drive-in where we knew a lot of our friends would be. They drove us through the parking lot honking and many friends stood outside their cars and applauded. We were a little embarrassed, but happy. Then they took us to our apartment.

We had rented a small efficiency apartment for the two weeks. That is the amount of time he would have before leaving for the necessary processing that was required before he left for Vietnam. I felt sick every time I thought about him going. Most of the time, I pretended that he wouldn't leave, and we would live happily ever after. It was a young heart in denial and the dream of a young girl.

We spent our two weeks visiting his family and our friends though I wanted him all to myself. He had such a good heart. One evening we were leaving to go have dinner with one of Dean's cousins and his wife. Two blocks from our little apartment, we saw a young couple pushing their broken-down car. Dean stopped to help them. There were no cell phones nor a pay phone nearby, so we took them to an auto parts store and bought a part they needed and a cold drink for all of us. Then we went back, and Dean installed the part. The couple said they were getting married soon. We wished them well and were on our way again. We were already late and then we got lost.

I felt bad that we didn't make it to have dinner with his cousin, but Dean's kind heart would not leave the young couple stranded. When we were alone we talked about our future, and the children we planned to have. "We'll have a girl with your hair and my eyes and we'll name her Stephanie," he said.

"And we'll have a boy who looks exactly like his daddy with wavy dark hair and we'll name him Donovan," I added. We had talked about those names many times before and it was decided. All the while I felt that dreadful ache in my heart for the time he'd have to leave me again and go into harm's way.

True to his word, he had learned several songs on his guitar. We would sit cross-legged in the middle of our bed as he sang love songs to me. I found out, much later, from one of his army buddies, that he stayed up late at night in the latrine at Fort Benning and practiced. Hank William's *"Cold, Cold Heart"* or Ray Charles' *"Here We Go Again"* and of course *"Together Again."* It brought tears to my eyes each time he sang, *"I'm so Lonesome I Could Cry."* He may never be a singing star, but in my eyes, Dean was the brightest shining star. We did make as much alone time as we could for laughing and loving one another. Those times are precious memories for me.

Too soon, the day for Dean to leave arrived. We had stayed our last night at his parents' house. Our parents, along with his brothers, drove us to the Hobby Airport the next morning. He held my hand with both of his hands as we waited for his boarding time. "I love you, Baby Cakes, I'll come back to you next July and sing *Together Again* to you forever." he whispered in my ear as he held me and kissed me. I trusted him with all my heart and was sure he would keep that promise. The pain I felt as the plane took off was unbearable. I didn't want to leave the airport; I just wanted the family to leave me there to wait for him to return. It felt like my heart was being ripped apart in my chest as I watched the plane disappear into the clouds.

We had been together for two years. I didn't know that we had shared our last kiss and it was the last time I would see him. He called me several times before he left from the States for his overseas flight. When he called the last time, I was anxious to tell him I thought that I might be pregnant. We were so excited and hopeful. His first letter was full of plans for our baby if it turned out that we would have a child while he was gone. We had talked many times about our children. He so wanted to be a dad and he would have been a good one.

A couple of weeks later, I had to write him that it was a false alarm. We were both so disappointed. Oh, how I wish that I could have given him a child. Yes, we were young, too young to be parents, but my life would have been so different with his child to care for. It would have been a part of him and his legacy. Maybe he would have been more careful if I had given him a child to come home to.

After Dean arrived in Vietnam, I never missed the news on television or the newspaper. I was constantly listening for 101st Airborne and looking for his face in the faces of the soldiers they filmed. I had never attended church much. The only thing I knew about the Bible was the Christmas story and the Easter story. But my dad had always talked about God as if He were real; therefore, I believed there was a God who answered prayers. I started to sometimes attend church services with Dean's mother. I prayed continuously for Dean to be safe. We were planning to meet in January for his R. & R. and I couldn't wait to see him.

One day in early October, Dean's parents came to my house. They both looked so solemn that I was afraid to hear what they were going to say. "Dean has been wounded," Mr. Whitlock told me. "He called us and asked us to tell you in person. He didn't want you to find out in a telegram or something. He is in a hospital in Japan."

"Thank you, God, that he is alive. He'll be coming home to me," I whispered through my tears. He called me twice from Japan. I was so happy to hear his voice, but when I asked him when he was coming home he said, "The wound isn't too bad; the army is patching me up and will send me back to my unit before too long."

"No!" I cried. "How can they do that?"

"I love you, Red. Let's just take what we have now. Don't stop writing to me, I couldn't do this without your letters," he said.

"Oh, Dean, My Love, I will never stop writing you. You are my life and I love you so much," I answered. Some days later, on my birthday, I received another phone call from him. We just kept saying how much we loved and missed one another. I wanted to reach out and touch him.

"Tell me what you want for your birthday, Babycakes?" he asked me.

"You are all I want for my birthday or any other time," I answered.

"I'll be home when I am done here," he whispered back to me.

I could hear the tears in his voice and I was openly crying. "Don't finish this call like this," I told myself.

"Bring me something silk from Japan but bring it to me in person. Dean, I love you so much. How can I bear these months without you? I pray for you," I said.

"You do? Don't stop praying, Baby and don't stop loving me."

"It was so hard to say goodbye again. The call was followed a few days later by a package with a pair of beautiful blue silk embroidered pajamas and a 101st airborne souvenir pillow. Sadly, we learned that his R. & R. had been exchanged for his time in the hospital. We would not be seeing one another after all.

I continued to write to Dean every day. He told me about some of the soldiers who received "Dear John" letters while in Vietnam. "You will never get one of those. Don't even think about it," I told him. I can't imagine the damage done to them with that kind of news. I did not want him to ever doubt my love for him or that I was faithfully waiting and praying for him. There was no one else for me from the night we met, when he smiled at me.

I received at least one letter from him every one or two weeks. I lived for those letters, my entire life revolved around them and my writing to him. I was counting the days until he would be home. I imagined all the things that could happen to him before that day. And I prayed.

I was still in school and my grades suffered greatly. I went from a B student to a C and D student. It just wasn't important to me anymore. My friends seemed so young to me and what they talked about was so insignificant. I avoided them as much as I could. My mind was completely focused on Dean and our future together.

12. Faithful In Love

I MET SAM WHILE DEAN WAS IN BASIC TRAINING. HE WAS IN THE navy and had come to visit his brother who was married to my cousin, Tessa. He knew how I felt about Dean. He asked me out while he was visiting them, but I told him that I had a boyfriend away in basic training. He didn't want to take no for an answer, so I told him, "I'm not interested in anyone except Dean. I love him, and he is the only guy that will ever be in my life."

He said, "Well, he's not here and I'll bet he isn't being faithful to you while he's gone."

That touched a nerve in me. Even after all this time, it was hard for me to believe Dean had chosen me, out of all the girls he could have picked. I was afraid he would one day see me the way I saw myself and change his mind about me. I avoided Sam the next few days until he left to go back to his ship.

The next time I saw Sam, was in August after Dean had left for Vietnam. He had come to his brother's house following their mother's funeral, which was in another state. The Navy had given him special leave. He said, "I wanted to ask you out again, but my brother told me that you married that boyfriend of yours. Are you still being faithful to him or will you go out with me?"

"I am married; I will always be faithful to him. Evidently you have never loved anyone except yourself. Please don't bother me again," I answered.

He couldn't understand that I wasn't interested in him, nor was I tempted. I introduced him to one of my friends from school and they dated a couple of times while he was in town. Before he returned to his ship, it left for Vietnam. He was transferred to another ship and never went to war.

Sam was so different from Dean. He was bad-mannered, foul-mouthed, and disrespectful. It didn't matter who was around, his language didn't change. He was exactly what I had heard sailors were like. He made crude jokes and bragged about all his drinking and the many girls he had. He was not my type at all.

When Dean had come home following Basic Training, I told him about Sam asking me out while he was gone. Dean asked, "So do you want to go out with him?"

I couldn't believe he would even ask me that, but I told him, "Absolutely not. I told him that I love you and would never want anyone else." I did not write to Dean about Sam asking me out the last time. I didn't want him to worry about that while he was in Vietnam. He needed to only think about how much I loved him and that I was here waiting for him to return.

I lived for Dean's letters telling me how much he loved and missed me. I continued to write him every day and sent packages whenever I could. He told me some of the guys were jealous of all the mail he received. He felt bad for the ones who rarely received mail from home, so he shared his packages with them. I'm sure all the guys did that kind of thing for one another.

The first week in January of 1967, I received two envelopes from Dean. They were filled with pictures, but no letter. Some of the pictures were of him and some other guys when he was in the hospital in Japan. He had told me when he called from Japan about a Japanese girl band that played country music and there were a couple of pictures of them and a guy country band. Many of the pictures were of him in the jungle and of the tents, camps, gear, weapons, and other soldiers working around the camp. There were some pictures of the jungle, trucks on a dusty road, and a river. It broke my heart to see how he was living, even though the pictures didn't tell half the misery over there.

I knew the war was changing him. How could it not? He looked older than his nineteen years. I had heard that the men were changed a lot when they came back. I didn't know what to expect but was hoping that my love for him would be enough to make him alright when he came home. I was anxious about how he would have changed and even wondered if he would still love me. Maybe he would decide he didn't want to be married after he came back. I just didn't know what to expect, but I never stopped loving, writing, or praying for him.

13. Till Death Do We Part — 1967

THE DAY I WAS NOTIFIED IS STILL A BLUR TO ME. IT WAS TUESDAY, January 10, 1967. It was a chilly morning and I was sitting in front of the fire while getting ready for school. I had not felt well the day before and stayed home from school. So, I had two letters for him beside me, one for yesterday and one for today. They were lying on top of my books for me to drop off at the mailbox on my way. I heard a car in the driveway, which was very unusual for that time of morning. It was my dad's day off and he was still sleeping upstairs. When I looked out the window, I saw two Army officers walking to the front door. I knew instantly. When I opened the door, one of the officers asked if I was Mrs. Whitlock. I don't remember answering them or hearing anything else except someone screaming, "Daddy, Daddy, Daddy!" I realized later that it had been my own voice that I was hearing.

My dad raced down the stairs. Everything is blank in my memory from that moment until my dad and I were walking up the sidewalk to Dean's parent's house to tell them. I remember his mother smiling when she saw me, and I started to cry. She screamed, "No!" We stayed until Mr. Whitlock got home. My dad then took me to my school to get his brother and to the middle school to pick up the other brother. We took them home. All I remember after that is someone giving me a Valium and at some point, my mother was there.

I don't remember going to my house, sleeping in my bed, or anything about that evening. My memory skips from lying on Mr. & Mrs. Whitlock's couch to another day where I was standing on the steps of a funeral home where they had taken Dean for viewing. I could not walk up the steps and go inside. Suddenly, Sheila, the girl Jamie had dated was holding my arm. We had become friends. She was talking softly to me and guiding me into the funeral home. It's strange to me how vividly I remember that she was wearing a leopard skin coat. When I saw him, I said, "It's not him! They made a mistake!" I tried to convince myself that it wasn't him, but it was my Dean. I remember thinking that we had married on a Tuesday and he had died on a Tuesday, seven months later.

The Army had assigned an officer, Major Eaves, to help me with all the arrangements and advise me of things I needed to do. He was also to give me the details of how Dean had died.

The next memory I have is sitting in the office at a different funeral home planning and arranging for the burial. Dean's dad did not want him buried at the Veterans' Cemetery, so it was in the cemetery near where we all lived. My parents and Mr. & Mrs. Whitlock were with me. I don't remember being at my house since the officers came to the door. I don't' remember if or where I slept or what day it was. I asked Dean's parents to help me make decisions on the arrangements, and they did.

I do not remember being at our house or anyone's house during that week. My memory is totally blank on many things, even after all these years, but I remember being next to Dean in that little room. I don't know how long I stood there over the glass sealed casket staring into his face, willing him to wake up. I spent the next three days next to him. I stayed as long as they would allow me to stay there. I only left him when the people were going to lock up. People tried to talk to me about rest and food, but I didn't even answer them. I fell apart so many, many times, but someone kept giving me Valium to keep me calm. I remember small fragments of time, such as one of his relatives, that I barely knew, sitting with me at the funeral home and holding me while I cried. I was so grateful to her and still think of her when that time comes to mind. I wish I could thank her. I remember one of his brothers breaking down while we were there. I do not remember who came and went, but I didn't want to talk to anyone. I knew that people were around me all the time, his relatives and mine, and our friends, but I wasn't always sure who was there. I didn't care who was there. No one could bring him back to me.

One evening on the way home, my mom took me to buy a dress for the funeral at the same store where I had purchased the white dress for my wedding. Had that been only eight months ago? I bought a black one.

The Army arranged for our two friends, Jamie and Bud, to be flown home from where they were stationed to be honorary pallbearers. Bud, I think, was at Fort Bliss in El Paso and Jamie was in the Army; I don't remember where he was stationed. Jamie was about to go to Vietnam. They were Dean's closest friends and I was glad they could be there.

The Army gave me a $10,000 check. "Is that what a soldier's life is worth these days?" I asked. What a cruel joke! I tried to give the check back to them, but they would not take it. Finally, my family and Dean's parents told me that Dean wanted me to have it. I didn't know it, but he had told my parents and his before he left that if he didn't come back that I would get the money and asked them to help me use it for myself. He had told me, the night before he left, to share a portion of the money with his parents and his aunt if he didn't come back. I had pushed that out of my mind because he had promised to come back to me. I did as he told me. It meant nothing to me. No amount of money could ease my pain or help me to cope without him. There was nothing or no one who could comfort me.

The Army provided a limousine to take me to the church for the funeral. I had never been in one before and I have no recollection of what it looked like now. The church was the one where Dean's mother was a member. The same minister who officiated at our wedding, officiated at his funeral. Outside the church, I saw Jamie and Bud standing at attention in their uniforms next to the hearse. Major Eaves was holding my arm guiding me to the limousine, but I pulled away and ran to them and hugged them both as I cried. I don't know if it was right or wrong to go to them while they were "on duty", but I needed my friends who loved both Dean and me. I know they were hurting, also. After a few minutes, the Major gently took my arm away from them and escorted me into the limousine and we were driven to the cemetery. I guess I thought if I held on to Jamie and Bud that I would wake up from this nightmare.

I remember the unbearable physical pain and that my legs were so weak they would hardly move. Putting one foot in front of another was like walking in quicksand. I had to be steadied on either side by two strong figures; I think it was my dad and mother. I was led to the chair next to Mrs. Whitlock and sat down. It was a cold, overcast day, January thirteenth, and the sky was full of dark gray clouds that promised a thunderstorm soon. It matched the way I felt in my heart. There was a hazy crowd of people around the open grave and the casket was a steel gray color and looked as cold as it was. It was covered with an American flag. There were hundreds, maybe thousands of flowers around us. I don't remember any of the words that were spoken that day. I do still remember the exploding sound of the twenty-one-gun salute and the haunting whine of Taps being played by the soldiers. The flag was ceremoniously folded by two soldiers, perhaps Jamie and Bud, but I'm not sure. Then one of them presented the folded flag to me. Every time I hear and see the ritual of a military funeral since that day, I cannot stop my tears.

Jamie was headed to Vietnam, but before he left to go back to his unit, he came to see me with one of Dean's brothers. I can't remember what we said to one another, but I do remember the comfort I received. It was almost as if Dean was there with us. Jamie and I had never visited together without Dean there. Someone took our picture together holding Dean's folded flag. I still have that treasure, though I lost touch with him when he left for Vietnam.

The week after the funeral, Major Eaves took me to Ellington Air Base to get a military ID and to introduce me to the commissary and the medical facilities there. About a month after the funeral, he escorted me to a special ceremony at the local Army Reserve Base, where there was a ceremony to posthumously present Dean's Purple Heart and Bronze Star with "V" for valor due to his heroism, to me, his widow. Besides these prestigious medals, he also was awarded the *Vietnam Service Medal*, *Republic of Vietnam Campaign Ribbon with Devices*, the *National Defense Service Medal*, the *Parachutist Badge*, the *Combat Infantryman's Badge*, and *Sharpshooter Badge with Rifle Bar*. None of these were much comfort, in fact it made me angry. I didn't need them to tell me how brave and honorable he was; after all, he had been my knight of honor, my protector, and my defender since I had known him. He was worth so much more than money and medals to me. There was an overwhelming emptiness and loneliness in my heart at the finality of it all. It was over, not just the funeral and presentation of Dean's medals, but also my life; the love of my life would never come home to me. What was I going to do without my Dean; he was the reason that my heart beat and my lungs breathed air in and out. Going on without him was incomprehensible. This had to be a nightmare and I would wake up soon.

14. Visiting The Silent Land — 2005

THE GROUNDS ARE AS PICTURESQUE AS EVER AND THIS SPOT
near the pond feels as comfortable as an old friend. In the pond, there
are swans and ducks that swim across the mirror-like water as if in
a dream. They will swim quickly to you, looking for food, when you
leave your car or go near the pond. A large fountain was added to the
center of the pond a few years ago, where before there had been a
small island. It was almost as if this section of the cemetery had stood
still in time, the place where I had left him so long ago. It is the only
place where I can sit quietly with my memories and talk to him; I had
done it every day in the beginning. In later years, I came only when I
could get away. It is so ironic that we had driven by this place so many
times when we were dating. Though the area has changed, I could still
pick out the little area where we would park when we came with our
friends. I never thought how much time I would spend here alone in
the coming years.

The "oldies" radio station in my car was playing Nino Tempo and
April Stevens as I pulled along the side of the narrow road near where
Dean was buried, just a few feet from the pond. It was the same spot
where I had parked countless times, only steps from my reason for being here between him and the pond. Nino and April sang on, *"As long
as my heart shall beat, sweet lover we'll always meet, here in my deep purple
dreams."* I remember singing along with this song on the radio in Dean's

car. Now it seems like it was words of prophecy to me as tears come to my eyes. How I loved him then and how I love him still.

Walking towards the grave, my mind was whirling with the hundreds of memories of this place. I felt a chill as I brushed the debris from the marker so that I could see the words written there: *Pfc. Alan Dean Whitlock; 1st Brigade, 101st Airborne; Born July 8, 1947 – Died January 10, 1967; Vietnam.* How long had I been bringing flowers to Dean's grave? How many times had I met with him there to tell him that I still loved him? How long had it been since anyone else had been here? His dad had passed away in 1984 and was buried next to him. His mother was buried next to his dad. She had died in 2000. I had not seen Dean's brothers in many years. I don't know if they visited his grave.

During the years when I couldn't go, my cousin, Darlene, would take flowers to him for me. I had brought flowers for Dean's mother also and put them in her vase. His dad's marker has no vase, so I place an American flag in the ground next to it. I always had an American flag in Dean's vase; he loved his country. I guessed that most of his close family members, except his brothers, were gone by now. Besides his parents, I knew his aunt, his grandmother, and his cousin that he had lived with, had passed away and were buried in this cemetery, though I don't know where.

I wanted it to look like someone cared enough to bring flowers even after so many years. I also wanted to be near him; though I knew he was not there, I had no other place to go but the place where I had left him. Almost all the places we used to go were gone, replaced by other unfamiliar structures. The house I lived in while we were dating burned down several years ago. Most of our friends have passed on or I have lost touch with them. My memories and my love for him are as strong as they have ever been.

As I stand beside his grave, I know my vow to him on our wedding day, to love him until the last beat of my heart, will never be broken.

Death has not changed my feelings for him, if anything, they have intensified. I thought of the night before Dean left for Vietnam when he said, "Red, if something happens and I don't come back I want you to use the insurance money to make a better life for yourself. You deserve to live a good life. That's what I want for you."

"Please don't talk about it. I can't think about that. You will come back!" I had answered. But I did think about it constantly in the next few months. Every day I lived with the fear of losing him, and then I did.

My mind went to the package and the pictures I had sent to him for Christmas a few weeks before he was killed, and how hard the holidays were for me because I knew they were terrible for him. I was so distracted thinking about him in that horrible jungle risking his life every day, that I couldn't eat or share in the family celebrations at all.

I thought about our plans for children, the names we had chosen for them, and the life together loving one another and how it would never be. He was so full of life with such a great sense of humor and a compassionate heart. It was so hard for me to understand how someone as good and young as he was could be taken when there are so many evil people in the world.

I thought about how I had prayed for God to keep him safe. I believed there was a God who could hear me when I prayed, but would He hear me and answer my prayer? I still think about those things so often. He never leaves my thoughts. Even now I want to ask God "Why?", but I know that He has a plan and even when we do not understand it, it is His perfect plan.

Dean loved his mother. He always called her "Momma." He was very protective of both of us and always spoke with respect to and about us. He teased the two of us because he loved to see us laugh. It wasn't a sarcastic kind of teasing, just natural humor. There was always a bond between his mother and me because of our shared love for him. All we had left of him was one another. Many times, I have wished she and I could just sit together and talk, but I could not. By the time my life was in a place where I was able to visit with her, I could not find her, and then she was gone.

There are things I would have loved to have, like his high school ring. I wore it more than he did, and it was special to me. I'm sure he left it with his mother. When he left for Vietnam, Dean took his mother's high school class ring with him for luck. She had asked him to take it because his dad had carried it with him through his tour of duty in WWII and he came back safely. When Dean's possessions came back with his body, his mother's ring was not with them. There was a picture of me that I had sent to him shortly after he left. He had folded it and it was worn and dirty from carrying it with him. On the back I had written, "I love you, "Red." (I confess)." My hair looked red in the picture and I confessed that his nickname for me was justified.

Many of the Vietnam Veterans that I have heard speak or have talked to myself, relay stories of their ongoing health issues from the chemicals they were exposed to in Vietnam. They have told stories of men who came back from Vietnam in body, but never in mind. Thousands of them, unable to cope with the memories, emotional pain, or physical pain, have committed suicide through the years. When I think of Dean possibly having to endure such a life, I wonder if I would have been mature enough to help him, even with the enormous amount of love I had for him. Failing him would be devastating for me. There were many who adjusted to their life at home, but the horrors these men witnessed is still impossible for them to forget.

The last time I saw him was when he got on the plane at Hobby Airport in Houston, Texas. The last time I heard his voice was a phone call from the 106th General Army Hospital in Yokohoma, Japan. The last call was on my birthday. My birthday has been a sad day for me since then. Most people don't know why I dread that day so much. I don't explain it. The last time I received mail from him was a few days before he died. It was the two envelopes filled with pictures from Japan and Vietnam.

There was no letter with the pictures, as I said. I was very disappointed about that but thought I would probably receive a letter in the next day or two. I kept the pictures near me. In one of these pictures of him in a Vietnamese jungle camp, he had written words of love to me on the back as he did on some earlier pictures he sent from Fort Polk, and Fort Benning. He had such a great personality. I cherish each picture; it is all I have left of him.

I pause for a few more minutes beside his grave, feeling the soft breeze on my face and in my hair before returning to my car. "I still love you," I whisper. I can almost hear him whispering softly in the wind, "Hey, Red, I love you, too. Thanks for remembering me." As always, the tears are falling again as I walk to my car.

15. Confusion And Fear Rule — 1967

AS I SAID, AFTER DEAN'S DEATH I WOULD DRIVE TO THE CEMEtery every day after my last class and sit beside the duck pond across from his grave until dusk when they closed the gates. I felt peaceful there and could cry privately, with no one to try and comfort me. Everyone seemed to just go on with their lives as if this huge heartbreak had not happened; as if it didn't affect them at all. My world was dead. Sometimes my friends and family made me feel as though I should stop grieving. They acted as though we had just broken up like teenagers do. "Move on" they would say, "He wouldn't want you to be so sad." Eventually I began to hear rumors that were being spread at school that I was dating already, and Dean only gone a couple of months. Dean's brother became very distant and even hateful to me. I have no idea who started the rumors or why, or if that was the reason for his distance. Anyone who knew me would know it was a lie; I only stayed at home, went to school, spent time with my family, but mostly I spent my time alone. The rumors were completely false.

When I gave Dean my heart, it was his forever; even knowing he wasn't coming back, he still owned it. What could his brother be upset with me about? I have never known why. As if there wasn't enough anguish in my life, now I wanted to hide from everyone. If people only knew the hurt and long-lasting damage they do to a life when they gossip.

Once I asked my mother, "How long does mourning last?" She an-

74

swered that I should give myself a year; that time would help ease the pain. I guess she didn't know and just wanted to give me something to hold on to. As a sixteen-year-old, I didn't know how to process all the advice I was receiving. It seemed that everyone had an opinion as to what I "needed to do." So much of it was conflicting and I was very confused. I'm sure it hurt Dean's parents that I stayed away from them; I wanted and needed to be with them so badly, but I didn't know what his brother had told them and honestly, I was afraid of him and did not trust him.

I was on the edge of a nervous breakdown. No one seemed to understand that Dean had been my best friend, my warrior, my future, my breath of life, and that I couldn't live without him.

I could not eat and soon my weight was less than 100 pounds. The pain was so severe that I wanted to die. I had not only contemplated suicide, but I planned several ways to do it. It seemed like the perfect solution to end my pain. One day I was alone at home and I found myself standing in front of the bathroom mirror with a mouth full of Valium that I had collected from refilled prescriptions. I heard a car in the driveway outside the window and vomited when I tried to hurry and swallow them. My dad was a hunter and always had rifles and shotguns in the house. Though I was afraid of them, it was one of my plans. I guess my parents suspected my state of mind and they locked them up.

I had bought a new car with part of the insurance money. Dean's brother told me that Dean had talked about buying a new Ford Fairlane, black with red interior, so that is exactly what I bought in honor of him. Later, I wasn't sure if it was Dean's choice of a car or his brothers. Many times, I visualized myself driving over a bridge or into a tree in my car. I would drive extremely fast on lonely roads hoping that it would just happen. Wouldn't it be poetic justice to die in the car that I had bought with his life insurance money? I could never get the courage. I was afraid that I would not die, but only be permanently injured. After that, I only prayed that God would take me in His own way. But it seemed that God had other plans for my life.

One night I had a dream, or maybe it was a vision, if there are such things. It was very clear and real to me. Dean came to me. He took my hand and we walked through a very bright field, I didn't recognize anything around me. He told me not to cry, that he was alright. He told me that he was safe in this beautiful place. Then I saw that everything was indescribably beautiful and bright every direction I looked; I could not describe it. He told me that he was waiting for me there and that he loved me. I didn't tell anyone about this for many, many years, but it was somehow comforting to me. Several years later, when I began to learn about God, I read a description in the Bible of what heaven would be like. The description sounded exactly like the dream or vision I had had. I don't know if God does this kind of thing, but possibly I was so young and experiencing such a devastating time, that He was easing my heart and mind.

In the months that followed, I did the things that I was expected to do; I went to school, cared for my brother and sister, and helped with the household chores. Things seemed to be a little better at home with my family for a while. The alcohol problem had stopped, at least temporarily. I even went to summer school to get extra credits and graduate early. I hardly ever listened to music any longer. As much as it had been a part of me, I couldn't stand to hear it now. Even now I cannot listen to the music that was popular for many years after Dean was gone. The only time I wasn't pretending that things were o.k. was when I sat at the duck pond after school and on weekends, close to Dean. That is when I could relax my emotions and release my tears.

By the time summer arrived, I started to become angry. I was angry with Dean for dying. It didn't make sense to me, but that is how I felt. Dean always loved my long "red" hair, so in my anger, I had my hair cut short and dyed it black. Though I was doing it in anger, I think I chose to color it black because his hair was black. My mind was confused, I was afraid, and I was totally lost; I didn't feel like I belonged anywhere. Many things I did that summer were not like me at all. I would drive around for hours; sometimes late into the night and sometimes very fast. When I could get it, I would drink alcohol until my pain eased a bit. Of course, it was back in a few hours and I hated that I wasn't completely in control of myself when I was high. After a while I decided that wasn't the answer. Dean would have hated to see the way I was abusing myself.

One of my aunts came to visit during the summer with her family. She invited me to go home with them to Los Angeles. I had another aunt and uncle there also. Since I had finished summer school and it was a few weeks before the fall semester started, I decided to go. I enjoyed the visit and seeing everyone. I had cousins there that I had never met. We went to Disneyland and other tourist places and even looked for movie stars at the L.A. mall. It was a good distraction, but I was still sad, and it got worse after I returned to Texas.

School started and some of my friends were trying to fix me up with dates. I certainly wasn't ready for or interested in dating. Then I went for a long weekend in October to visit my friend Becky in Mississippi. It was good to see her, but she had surprised me with getting dates for us both while I was there. I didn't have a choice but to go. I'm sure the guy was nice, but he knew I wasn't interested in him. He said, "Becky told me about your husband. I think you are still missing him and you don't want to be here." I was drinking that night and didn't care about anything, but I just shook my head with tears in my eyes. The so-called *date* was over. Thankfully he was a nice guy, or things could have been bad for me.

When I returned home and back to school, it felt as if I was moving in a fog every day. I automatically walked to and sat in each of my classes, but I hardly talked to anyone. At home, it was the same. I did what I thought I was expected to do each day. Most days I would drive in my car wherever it took me; to the car wash, Dean's old neighborhood, by the places we used to go, but I always ended up back at the cemetery with him. I knew everyone was as tired of my grief, as I was. I was a lost soul, not knowing what to do without Dean. I couldn't see my future without him. I begged God to take me to him.

16. The Choices We Make

AFTER A YEAR, I FELT NO BETTER, JUST VERY SAD AND VERY AN-
gry. I felt like I was drowning in the grief and could see no end to it.
My hope was buried under layer after of layer of pain. Everyone was
shocked, including me, when I married Sam, fifteen months after Dean's
death. He had started writing to me ten or eleven months after Dean's
death, just after I returned from my visit with Becky. He was in the U.S.
Navy, stationed on the east coast. At first it was strange; he was so different from Dean or any guy I knew. But his letters were another distraction
from the sadness that permeated my life. I had moved with my family
to another part of the city when he came to visit his brother for Thanksgiving. He wanted to see me; it wasn't a big deal to me, so I picked him
up in my car and we went to dinner. I saw him a couple of times and he
kept trying to impress me with how cool he was. After he went back to
his ship, he began calling and a few days after the New Year he called
me from New York and asked me to marry him. My grief was so overwhelming without hope of Dean coming home to me. I just wanted the
pain to end. I asked, "Sam, why do you want to marry me? Don't you
know I don't love you enough to marry you? I'm not even over Dean."

"I have loved you since the first time we met. I have enough love for
both of us. I just want to take care of you," he answered. To be taken care
of sounded so good to me. Isn't that what Dean had done?

I just wanted to stop the anguish I felt, so I agreed to marry him. It wasn't long before I knew I didn't want to marry him. Sam was due to be discharged from the Navy in April, so I knew I wouldn't have to see him for several months. Then his discharge came through early and he moved to Houston the end of January 1968. When he pressed me for a wedding date, I told him that I didn't want to get married before graduation and that August might be a good time. My plan was to break it off with him before graduation and then we would go our separate ways.

Dean's brother and I were in the same graduating class. Since he had begun to treat me like he hated me a few of months after Dean's death, the dirty looks and hateful remarks in the hallways each day were too much for me. I was even afraid of him, or what he might do. In March I dropped out of school. It was only two months before graduation, but I was facing one class to make up in the summer. I did eventually finish school and got my diploma, but looking back, I can see that I was making one bad decision after another.

My parents were not in favor of me dating Sam, and certainly did not want me to marry him. It was an argument with them every time I saw him. My dad even took my car keys once to keep me away from him, but I was so lonely. All my friends were tired of being around me and my suffering. The arguing was escalating with my parents and one night Sam said, "Let's get married this weekend." I was so tired of the arguing and worrying about where I was headed. I was confused with people on every side still giving me advice day after day. At first, I told him that I still didn't love him enough to marry him, but he persisted, so I told him alright.

I'm sure some professional counseling was in order for me, but who knew at that time? The night before we married, I told my parents. We fought, and I cried most of the night. My life was like a living hell. I didn't realize that my pain would not end with this decision, but that it would be increased.

We had the ceremony in a judge's office the next day. When we left the courthouse, I sat next to him in the car thinking, "What have I done?" I felt panic rising in my chest and I didn't know how to fix it. I did not want to be married to him. No matter what I did, people would be hurt. I had always been the one in the family to make everything alright when things were bad, but I didn't know how to fix my own problems.

Every night, for at least the first year, I would sit in the living room chair by the window and cry for hours after Sam was asleep. I cried for my Dean and felt so much guilt because I believed I was being unfaithful to him. I cried for the pain I had caused Dean's parents. I cried for what I was doing to Sam. I honestly didn't think the marriage would last; in truth, I was constantly trying to figure out how to get out of it. The choice I made was a bad one for many reasons. The biggest reason was that I was still in love with Dean and still grieving.

I have learned a lot about the grief process since then. Now I can see that I was in the "anger" stage of grief when I married Sam. I wanted everyone to hurt the way I was hurting. I was angry at the war, I was angry at Dean for dying, I was angry with Sam for not being Dean, I was angry with myself for being so weak, and I was angry with God. For someone who has not been through it, it may sound crazy, and maybe it was. I just was not ready to move on, but my "actress self" kicked in, as it always has in stressful situations, and I became Sam's wife. I would keep Dean in a private closet in my mind and my heart and take him out when I was alone. He never left my thoughts.

After we were married, Sam did not allow me to mention Dean or anything about that time in my life. If he discovered that Dean's mother had called me, we had a big fight. I was not allowed to see or talk to the friends I had known for years because they knew Dean. Many of my friends married, died, or had close family die in the first few years of our marriage, and I could not contact them. He wanted me to behave as if Dean and I had never happened; to act like I had no life at all before we were married. I eventually sent the ceremonial U.S. flag and Dean's medals to his parents. It was very hard for me to do, but it didn't seem right for them to be in storage at my parents' house when they could have them.

I felt perpetually guilty because I had to hide my memories. I felt I was betraying Dean and lying to Sam all the time. If I had a chance, I would go to visit Dean and write poems or notes to him and when I got home my "actress self" would emerge and I would cook dinner and be a different person when Sam came home. Those times were not often, because he took our only car to work each day and I was stuck at home alone. I didn't get to go out much. I lived in dread of the time when Sam would confront me about my feelings for Dean. But it never happened. I guess he didn't need to confront me because he already knew.

There were many problems in our marriage. We had nothing in common; there was nothing that we both liked. Our opinions always clashed, which caused more stress between us. We hardly knew one another at all. After the first year, we discussed what we wanted to do about our marriage. We finally decided to stay together, but my heart was not in it. I could never put Dean behind me. Though we never spoke about Dean or my feelings for him, Sam knew.

17. Moving On For Better Or Worse

OUR SON WAS BORN TO SAM AND ME TWO AND A HALF YEARS AF-
ter we married; I was almost twenty years old. My son became my focus. I prayed constantly that there would not be a war when he was old
enough to go and fight. Thankfully, God answered that prayer.

Sam had started staying away from home, going out with his friends
from work. Since we only had one car, I was left alone with the baby
most of the time. It finally escalated to the point that we were talking
seriously about divorce. Then I discovered that I was three months pregnant. So, once again we decided to stay together. Six days before our son
was two-years-old, our first daughter was born, and she was beautiful.
My children were like a dream come true for me. Love flowed from me
like I had never imagined. Both of our children were born in July. I was
anxious during both pregnancies that Sam would find out that Dean's
birthday was in July and there would be more angry words between us.
He didn't want anything that would remind me of Dean.

Being a mother instilled a kind of love in me that I had not expected
or experienced before, and it was beautiful. Because of these two precious
babies, I made the decision to try to make the marriage work. Sam had
made that choice before I did because he loved me. We both loved our
children and wanted them to have both a mother and a father to raise
them.

One day my mother asked Sam to get some things out of her attic.

When he came down, he had a large box of letters that Dean had written to me. My mom had saved them for me. I had not seen them since I married Sam. He put them in our car and we went home. I was dreading the fight I knew was coming. As I put the babies down for a nap, he took my letters in the back yard and burned all of them and a few pictures. When I realized what he was doing, I was horrified. He was so full of jealousy and rage. Instead of burning them out of my memory, as he thought he was doing, it just made me hate him. Here I was twenty-two years old, two babies, no job experience, and desperate to get out of a marriage from a man I hated. If Dean could see me now, what would he think? I was miserable, but the only choice I could see for myself and my children was to stay with Sam. It was not a happy marriage for either of us for many years.

I always had dreams about Dean. It was as if I had him back for that short time. Most of them I could not remember, I assumed because of the guilt I felt. After a while the dreams about Dean were very vivid and they happened more often. In every one of them the Army had made a mistake and he would come home and just show up at my front door to get me. I would open the door and fall into his arms and say, "We're *together again.*"

He would ask, "Why didn't you wait for me; I promised you I would come back."

"They told me you were gone forever," I would answer.

"I will never leave you again," he would promise.

Though I was remarried and even after we had children, in these dreams I would leave them all and go away with Dean. I had the dreams for about ten years, and then the dreams changed some. Dean would still come home to me, but I would wake up before I decided to leave my family or stay. Those dreams lasted for about seven years. I would be very sad the next day or two.

At this point in my life, I began the grieving process all over again as if it had just happened. This has happened several times since then. Seventeen years after Dean was killed, I started having vivid memories of mine and Dean's life together and of Dean's death and the events that followed. I had always felt sad and cried many times when something reminded me of him, but this was different; it was daily and seemed to be unending. It took all my strength and energy to take care of my children and my home.

Sam knew something was wrong, but he didn't ask. I'm sure he knew it was about Dean. I avoided him as much as I could. I cried all the time and spent every minute that I could get away from my family at the cemetery with Dean. That's when the dreams started again.

In the next phase of my dreams, I would not leave my children to go with him and he would look at me with pain and tears in his eyes and then leave me. I would change my mind as I saw him leave and try to follow him or find him. In the dream, I would see him in places we used to go, but I could not get to him. I knew he was gone from me forever this time. I would wake up feeling lonely and extremely sad on those mornings. On those days again, if I could get away, I would go and sit with him and my memories for a while.

Eventually I handled this the way I had always done, I stuffed it away inside me and became the actress again. Grief was too much for me to live with, so all I could do was become whomever I needed to be to get through the day, the week, the year, or my life.

I continued to be miserable in our marriage even though I was determined to stick it out. Sam was working every day, going to school three nights each week, and playing softball on weekends. We argued all the time and neither of us were happy. Gradually he stopped going out at night with friends because he was so busy with other things. I had no friends, and with Sam's many activities, I was left at home with the babies most of the time. Sometimes on Saturday, my mother would come over for coffee and a visit, but she worked all week and had things to do on the weekends. I was very lonely. Since we only had one car, if I needed it for an appointment with the doctor or something, I would take Sam to work and pick him up when he got off work. On those days, I would visit my grandmother and Dean if I had time. She had always been my rock and I missed her. Though I didn't confide in her and we never talked about it, she knew I wasn't happy.

Sam continued his jealousy. He didn't want me to have any friends apart from him. I'm sure he felt like he was second choice and, in truth, he was. I had not given him a thought when Dean was alive or for the year after he was gone. He retaliated by trying to destroy everything I had that he thought would remind me of Dean. What he didn't understand was that it was impossible to take away my memories of Dean. The places we went, songs on the radio, movies we had seen together, anniversary dates of our wedding and other special times, birthdays, and old friends that I would see at the mall or a restaurant. He was treasured in my heart and my mind forever. I could not forget him, nor did I want to. It seemed the more Sam tried to take away, the more I held on to my precious memories, and the more resentment I had for him.

One of my biggest regrets is that my bad choices hurt Dean's family and eventually it hurt Sam, our children, and all my relationships. I continued to be extremely angry, having fits of rage. Only through months of therapy have I learned to use a different thought process to control the rage, but I still felt the anger inside me.

18. Finding God

WHEN OUR DAUGHTER WAS ALMOST FOUR, I BECAME PREGNANT again, but I lost the baby in my fifth month. I was devastated. There were other disappointments at the same time. We lost out on an opportunity to buy a house that I wanted, and we had to quickly find a place to live while we searched for another one. I was so unsure of my life and our future, so I began searching for some answers. Why was I here? I believed there was a God, but I had no idea how to find Him. I had been angry with God for so many years that I didn't know if I wanted to search for Him. I had prayed many times each day for Dean to come home safely, but I felt like God took him away from me.

One day I screamed, "God, what do You want from me. Am I being punished because of my marriage to Sam?" I started praying passionately to whomever may be listening in heaven or wherever. I was searching through books and on television for some answers. My search took me in some unusual cult-like directions. I was very confused and fearful of what I might find. I was even wondering if maybe God was a myth and not real at all. Nothing was making sense to me; none of the things I was reading satisfied my longing for relief from the mess I had made of my life.

It was during this time in our marriage, we learned that we were having another baby. Two months into my pregnancy, I met a Christian woman who asked if she could study the Bible with me. For some reason I cannot explain, I told her yes. She came to my home with another woman from her church. I learned they were from a church that I had attended a couple of times with a neighbor that I had met when my son was a baby. This neighbor had befriended me in the beginning of our marriage when we were fighting so much. She moved across the state and I didn't go back to her church.

During my study with these two women, I learned about peace and about salvation through Jesus Christ. I know now they were sent by God as an answer to the prayers I had been praying for more than a year. The things she showed me in the Bible were comforting and filled me with hope as nothing ever had. I was baptized the first day we studied. Even though my morning sickness was making me want to stay home, the first Sunday morning after my baptism, the kids and I went to worship service.

When we came home, Sam was working around the house. He said to me, "If you are going to do this, I'm not going to stay home alone every Sunday and work." I told him we were going, and he could go with us or not. So, he went with me and he started making friends with the Christians there. I didn't make friends that easily, but I was excited about the things I was learning.

The more I studied the Bible, the more I knew that Jesus was the answer I had searched for all my life. Sam noticed that I was more at peace, except for the morning sickness which lasted until my eighth month. He began to study the Bible with a couple of the men from church and two months later, Sam was baptized. He said he wanted that peace that I had found in God. We were hoping that this new peacefulness in our lives would bring us closer to one another, and it eventually did.

We were looking for another house to purchase, but before we found one, Dean's young cousin, Carrie, that he and I had played with when she was about five-years-old, moved into the house next to us. She recognized me right away. Then Dean's parents came to visit her. What if Sam found out? I was in a panic. I'm sure I seemed rude to her in my fear. What if he discovered who she was. We found a house soon after that and moved away. If only I could see her now and explain.

Our marriage was not great because Dean was always between us. I couldn't let him go and Sam was still so jealous. He knew the times he found me crying or if I became very quiet and withdrawn that something had reminded me of Dean, but we never talked about it. I would get away from the house alone occasionally and sneak to the cemetery to visit with Dean for a little while. The guilt I felt on those days was crushing.

Neither of us knew what to do about the issues between us, so we ignored them. I resolved to make fun times for the kids. I wanted them to have better memories of their childhood than I did of mine. Sam started playing softball on the church league and the kids and I would go watch the games. I made several friends among the other wives and began to enjoy the times we spent together. Our third child, second daughter, was born a few months later. She seemed to make my life complete, but I guess God wasn't done with us; two years later we had our third daughter, fourth child. I was still amazed that I had so much love inside me to give. I didn't realize that I was using the love for my children to fill the void in my heart left by Dean's death. The children were my life.

It was a lot of work caring for the children and trying to train them to be responsible, honest people who believed that God should be an important part of their lives. Sam worked hard to provide for us. Neither of us wanted me to work while the children were growing up, so we lived on one income. Eventually, he was asked to be a deacon in the church and he accepted. God brought us closer to one another as we both raised our children, but we knew the issue was always there just under the surface, unresolved. Though I tried to make our lives happy and what I thought a nice Christian family should be, something was missing.

The reality was that part of me had died with Dean. I never felt like I was completely there with my family. Most pictures taken of our family, I am absent. There are very few pictures of me. I took the pictures because emotionally I felt disconnected. If I felt that way, then they surely could feel it also. I knew that Sam was aware of it. I was angry so much of the time and didn't always have a reason for it. I always chalked it up to monthly irritability and even believed it was, but at times I wondered about it. My friends didn't seem to suffer with that kind of anger.

Dean's mother was going with a group of American Gold Star Mothers to see the Vietnam Memorial Wall in Washington D.C. She invited me to go with them. I wanted to go so badly, but of course it was impossible. I didn't want her to know how I wasn't allowed to openly remember Dean, so I told her that I couldn't leave my children. All I could think of the next week is that I should be with her.

It was during the sixteenth year of our marriage that the *Traveling Vietnam Memorial Wall* came to the Houston area. I secretly went to see it since I thought I would never have an opportunity to see the one in Washington. I didn't tell Sam that I had gone. Seeing Dean's name on that wall and the picture they had there of him sent me into a dark depression.

I tried to hide from Sam the agony I was feeling. I found it hard to care for my kids and house. I didn't feel that I could talk to anyone about it because I didn't want to hurt Sam or the children. One day he found one of the poems I had written to Dean and he was very hurt and angry. I thought, once again, it would be the end of our marriage, but I knew Sam would never leave.

I started talking to a minister friend. He talked with me and prayed with me for a few weeks. He encouraged me to pray every time those depressing feelings started to return and to pray for my marriage. Slowly I began to be less depressed. It took about a year to get back to a somewhat normal state of mind, although occasionally I would get very emotional and go to the cemetery and drive by some of the places Dean and I would go. There were fewer and fewer of the places that reminded me of Dean and eventually there was only the cemetery. I knew it would hurt Sam if he knew, but I could not stop myself from going. Even after Sam found the poem, we still did not address our problems about Dean. He did not want to talk about it and I didn't want to fight. This is how we rocked on from year to year as our children grew up.

19. *Opening Wounds And Closing Doors*

WE DID STAY TOGETHER EVEN WITH OUR PROBLEM STILL BE-
tween us. We did a pretty good job of ignoring it and living our day to
day life in make-believe. Our children grew up; three of them went to
college, and the youngest was still in high school. Our son married a very
sweet girl and they were expecting our first grandchild, a boy. We were
both so excited at the prospect of becoming grandparents.

Just before our twenty-ninth anniversary, Sam was in the hospital for
knee replacement surgery. He didn't want the nurses to take care of his
personal needs, so I stayed with him during the day for the eight days he
was there. We had several profound talks about our children and a house
we were planning to build near my mother when he was fully recovered.
We also talked about our daughter's graduation the next month and her
wedding coming up in three months. We talked about our first grandchild due to be born soon and the plans we had for him.

Sam had a diseased heart, but he worked in the Houston medical
center, so it was convenient for him to walk over to visit his cardiologist
without me. He said it wasn't a big deal and his doctor had it all under
control. One day when I was there in his hospital room he said, out of
the blue, "I need to ask you to forgive me."

"Okay, for what?" I asked him.

"Please don't say anything until I'm finished okay?" he said.

"I'm listening," I said. I had no idea what he was going to say.

"I'm sorry that I've tried to erase Dean from your memory all these years. I was wrong for being so jealous and destroying his letters and other things that reminded you of him. I also told you that my brother told me Dean was unfaithful to you just before he went to Vietnam. That was a lie and I know it hurt you. I wanted you to hate him, but instead it just hurt you. Dean was an important part of your life. I know that you loved him very much; I just wanted you to love me that way. Now I know that nothing I did could destroy your memories. I know now that I shouldn't have pressured you into getting married. We should have waited until we knew one another better and maybe you could learn to love me. Can you forgive me for all I've done?"

I was not prepared for the things he was saying. It was so strange even hearing Sam speak Dean's name. I didn't know what brought this to his mind. Of course, I started to cry, but I didn't fall into his arms with words of love and forgiveness. I was so angry that he admitted that he had lied to me. He knew how hurt I had been all these years and he just let it smolder and grow. He had taken my entire life and molded it into what he wanted it to be. I had given up my friends that I had known for years and Dean's family because of him and his lies.

I was glad that he finally accepted the fact that I had a life and love before him, but did he expect me to just forgive him on the spot? I didn't know how to answer him. I said, "Sam, do you have any idea of the pain you have caused, not only for me, but for Dean's parents? I never believed that Dean was unfaithful to me because we were together constantly from the time we married until he left for Vietnam. But it hurt to hear that your brother would say that. Do you realize the hate I have had in my heart for you?"

"Yes, believe me I know the pain I have caused," he answered.

Of course, he knew. I would never let him call me "Baby" or would rarely allow him to kiss me or to hold me in public. Those intimacies belonged to Dean. I'm sure he knew when I pulled away from him when he wanted to hold me, that I was thinking of Dean.

"I know as a Christian, I have to forgive you, but I need you to give me some time. I appreciate that you have worked hard to make a good life for our family, but I need some time to digest this and pray about it. I have to leave right now; we'll talk about it again later," I told him.

I didn't know how to feel. I cried because it was too late to make up for distancing myself from Dean's family. His dad had passed away and I didn't know where his mother was. I loved her and missed her so much. I totally lost touch with all his family. I'm sure they thought I deserted them in their grief. My tears were for the anger and the hate I had allowed to grow in my heart for all these years because of what Sam had done. The damage that was done to so many people, including my children, could not be undone or even repaired. All these lives suffered because of his jealousy. How was I going to find enough forgiveness in my heart for him?

Sam was released from the hospital and three weeks later, on May 8, 1997, he had a fatal heart attack. He was fifty-years-old. I think he knew it was coming soon and that is why he needed to ask my forgiveness. I learned that his doctor wanted to put him on the heart transplant list, but that Sam was putting it off. We had not talked about his confession again because he was still healing from his surgery and I was busy with preparations for a graduation, a new grandbaby, and a wedding. It would be a private discussion and some of our kids were always around. Now I would have to learn to forgive him without him even being here.

My world changed drastically. Here I was a widow for the second time and only forty-six years old. I wasn't sure what I would do; our one income was now gone, and I had not had a job since high school. But I learned that Sam had prepared well for me to be taken care of until I could get a job. He had insurance that paid off our mortgage and life insurance that would last for a good while.

Our grandson was born three weeks after the funeral, and they chose to use Sam's favorite name for him. God blessed me to be able to stay home and care for him for a year while his parents worked. It was instrumental in helping me through the monumental events taking place in a short amount of time. I planned to start college classes in the fall so that I could get a job.

Our daughter had her wedding eight weeks after the funeral. We had ordered the invitations before Sam died and we sent them out after, with his name on them. Her brother escorted her down the aisle and there was not a dry eye in the church building. It was a very emotional day for us all. Watching my children mourn for their dad was hard for me. I canceled the house we planned to build and, in the fall I started night classes at the community college.

The next summer I moved to a nice neighborhood in a small community north of Houston. I got a job in a school library in the day time and kept up with my college classes at night and on weekends. I even took classes in the summer semesters. It was a big house and my two older daughters lived with me. They had good jobs and we lived together like roommates.

I had learned to use a computer and took a creative writing class and a speech class. The teachers of each of these classes encouraged me to continue my writing. These classes helped me to get a position in the office of the school where I was working. The next year I was hired by the church where we had worshipped since the children were babies. I became the Office Secretary, working with the church leaders and the ministers. Soon after, my daughters /roommates, married; one moved away from Houston and the other lived not far from me. I was fifty years old and alone for the first time in my entire life. I was terrified that I would not be able to make it on my own.

It didn't take me long to become so busy with my day to day life that I had no time to worry about how I could do it. My kids were a tremendous help to me. They spent time with me and even helped me financially while I was adjusting to all the changes. I stayed in the larger house for a couple more years and decided it was too big for me. The maintenance was more than I wanted to handle alone. I had a house built in another suburb of Houston and moved again. Time passed, and I was lonely. My first solution was to get a dog. She was a mix, German Shepherd and Malamute, named Kai. I kept her inside and she began to grow, but soon she became too large for me to handle when we walked so I found her a new home. I had five grandsons and a granddaughter by then and they were my salvation.

20. A Missed Anniversary — 2016

JUNE 7, 2016 WOULD HAVE BEEN MINE AND DEAN'S FIFTIETH AN-
niversary and January 10, 2017, it was fifty years since he was killed.
We never celebrated an anniversary together since we were married only
seven months when he was killed. Most people who know me do not
know how I still grieve over him after all these years. My old friend
Becky asked me recently on social media, "Do you still think about him
and wonder what your life would be like if he had returned?"

My answer was, "Every day of my life." That thought had never left
my mind. All through the remaining years of the war and after it was
over.

Like many others that grew up during the sixties and seventies,
thoughts associated with Vietnam have rarely left my mind. The protests
in colleges across the nation, news coverage each night on television, ref-
ugees "boat people", politics, music, assassinations, POW/MIAs, and the
KIA reports kept Dean on my mind constantly. But he had been in my
thoughts every day since the night I met him.

In 1973, I stood in the doorway of my living room, as Sam was
watching the POWs and all the soldiers returning home on the television news. I felt like screaming and wailing each time I saw these women
running to be reunited with their men on the tarmac. I had dreamed of
that scene for Dean and me so many times. Why couldn't I have had my
guy back, too? I could not stop my river of tears. I cried for their pain and

for their joy; I cried for Dean's sacrifice, I cried for what I had envisioned for us if he had come home. What a blessing for the families who had waited for word of their loved ones.

I thought about the contempt and disrespect shown to our soldiers returning from their tour of duty and how Dean would have been so hurt by that. The shameful behavior of some Americans hurt all the soldiers, families of soldiers, and our country. I thought about how I had been determined to stand by him on his return, no matter how he might have been changed by his experiences there.

I don't think anyone could comprehend the depth of my love for him. Yes, I was very young, but I knew that I loved him with all my heart. My heart still aches for him and the only thing I can think when he is heavy on my mind is, "I want him back, Lord," though I know it can't be. Sometimes, when I think of our love and wonder how our life together might have been, I visit the cemetery. I also now know that Dean died for me; yes, for his country and the people of Vietnam, but specifically for me. Our conversation the night before he left for New York then on to Vietnam was about what I was to do if he did not return. He had a plan and explained that I would have his insurance money and I was to use it to get a car and an education to make a better life for myself. He had designated me as his beneficiary before we were even married. If he did come back, he would take care of me and keep me safe forever after.

I now understand that is why he insisted that we not wait to get married but do it before he left. During his training, the men had all been instructed to get all their paperwork in order, including legally naming who their beneficiary would be. As I said before, he had a plan. He was an honorable and loving young man. He never again saw his country or the people who loved him, and whom he died for.

Dean was young, but like me, had been forced to grow up faster than either of us should have. We understood one another and, in our love we held on to each other. Death separated us physically, but he is with me, always, in my memories and in my heart. I have imagined that one day, in some way I would be with him again. I even wrote a poem many years ago, when I was still a young woman, about meeting with him. It is not what I wished for, but only thoughts that have come to me in the years without him.

Waiting Inside

She sits alone in her quiet room,
Seeming to wait for eternity.
Callers think her mind is gone,
That she's lost touch with reality.
Oh, but if only they knew,
Her mind is still aware.
She must wait inside herself,
And make the world a blur.
Inside, she is young again
Deep inside her mind
She relives her younger years
The precious, happy times.
That's when he came into her life;
The summer of her thirteenth year.
He had such a charming smile,
He dispelled all her fears.
He was tall and so strong
She'd never been loved so much
He was her "Knight in shining armor"
And he had a gentle touch.
She loved him with all her heart
And at fifteen became his wife
Then on a cold, rainy, winter's day,

The war took his young life.
It was only seven months
Since he had left her back home
The love of her life would not return,
Oh, if only she could go.
But God's plan was for her to live
Though she prayed He'd take her life
After too short a time,
She became another's wife.
She lived her new life
With caring and contentment
She bore four precious children
And knew they were heaven sent
She couldn't love with all her heart
Though she tried to give
A part of her, on that winter's day
Had forever ceased to live.
She gave to her sweet family,
All she had left to give.
They just couldn't always understand
How hard it was to live
There were times when she felt the guilt
For depriving her sweet family
Of a wife and mother who could share,
All of herself, completely.
When at last she could give no more,
It seemed her mind was gone.
She settled into a private world,
Where she could feel at home.
In this world of hers alone
He visits with her there

She tells him of the years they missed
And how she always cared.
She tells him of her love for him
How it never, ever ceased
He tells her that he was with her there
And how his love increased.
In her mind she can see
The two of them at peace
He holds her in his arms
She knows this will never cease.
Now she sits alone in her mind
With a quiet peaceful smile
Knowing that she'll go to him,
In a very little while.

But, there is more to my story. Much to my surprise, this was not the end of my love story. A true love story never ends. It had not been resolved and still lingered in my mind. There was no resolution with Sam and it was hovering over me all the time.

21. Like Living In A Nightmare

I HAD LIVED ALONE FOR SEVENTEEN YEARS. MY MOTHER WAS ALSO living alone in the house she and my dad had built. It was located about twenty miles outside the city in a country setting near the lake. She was growing older and not able to drive any longer, so she decided to sell her house and live in town with her younger sister, who was recently widowed. I was surprised when Mother called me one day while I was shopping. "Do you want to buy my house; I'd like to keep it in the family?" she asked. There are a couple of acres of land with the house and she offered a good deal on it. I knew she was going to sell it, but thought my brother was buying it. She said he had changed his mind.

"Mother, I don't know what to say. Let me think about it for a few days," I said. I was sure I did not want to buy it, but since I had given my life to God, I knew it was not my decision to make alone. I asked God for His guidance in this.

I had a house I had bought when it was new; it was only ten years old. I told God that I really didn't want to buy her house, but I would do whatever He led me to do. After more than a week, I had no clear answer, so I decided to put my house on the market. I didn't think it would sell but, if it did I would know that is what God wanted me to do. If not, I would stay in my house. It sold in six days. It seemed a clear answer to my prayer that I was to buy my mother's house. It has been my experience that God can be very clever in His answers. I continued to tell

102

God that I really didn't want to do this and if He blocked the sale and purchase in some way I would know this wasn't His plan. Many times, I prayed for God to change His mind and let me stay in my house, but it just escalated out of my control. After the appraisal of my mother's property, I told Mother that I could not afford to buy it…she lowered the price. Everything went smoothly with the selling and purchasing. I was buying my mother's house and moving to the country, against my will, but evidently it was God's plan.

All my mother's furnishings and things she didn't have room for when she moved had to be disposed of before I could fit all my things into the house. She left her dishes, utensils, pots and pans, sheets, towels, books, pillows, documents, decorations, furniture, everything. I felt things were moving too fast; my mind was spinning, and my body was exhausted.

It was a huge job along with the preparations to ready the house for me and the actual move. My daughters and daughter-in-law pitched in and practically did it for me. I cleaned top to bottom and they painted the entire inside of the house and helped me move things out and in. Almost before I knew what was happening, I was living in the country by the lake with deer roaming through my yard; my son and his family lived in the house on the next property. They had built a house on the land where Sam and I had planned to build. As peaceful a setting as it was, when I was settled, the anger that I had been accumulating inside my heart for many years, began to seep out more and more. It seemed that I had been angry most of my life; more specifically since Dean had been killed. The number of people I had offended with my anger is hard to say.

Once again, I felt that my life was being manipulated and I was physically and emotionally worn out. My anger was aimed towards anyone who was in my path. I began to alienate people I had known and loved for a long time, including my children. I was completely out of control and severely depressed. I did not care if I lived or died at that point. I pleaded with God to take me. I didn't want to hurt my family any longer.

Finally, I mentioned it to my doctor and told him I felt like I was suicidal, he told me to talk to my son right away so he could help me find a good therapist that was on my insurance plan. I called him that night and my son helped me find a woman who worked with adult children of alcoholics. That was perfect. She was wonderful. I learned how my fear and anger was typical characteristics of these adult children. I guess that means that I was normal in a strange kind of way. I am so thankful to this woman who taught me how to change my thought pattern when the darkness appeared.

I was in therapy for six months when my therapist suggested that I didn't need to see her any longer. I was a little uneasy about going it alone, but she assured me that I had learned all the skills I needed to control my anger and my fears; skills that could mend the relationships I had damaged. She told me that she would be available at any time if I needed to call her.

I moved what was left of Mother's furniture into the garage and started advertising it to sell. I began drawing plans for landscaping and some changes inside the house. One night as I was packing some of her things to donate to a charity, I found a box on the top shelf of a closet. Inside I discovered that Mother had kept hidden some of my pictures of Dean and me, including four wedding pictures, a few pictures of us when we first started dating, and the pictures he had sent me from Vietnam just before he was killed. Under these I found my wedding band. I didn't remember her saving these for me and she had said nothing about it. I guess she decided to wait until I asked her. It had been forty-eight years. I touched the pictures and placed the wedding band on my finger.

Tears filled my eyes, but then I saw that some of the pictures had writing on the back. Dean had written names of some of his brother soldiers on the backs and then I saw the greatest treasure of all. He had written words of love to me on the back of some of them. Slowly through the years I had started to doubt that Dean loved me as much as I loved him. It had been so long since I had seen these pictures that I had completely forgotten about them. I assumed they had been destroyed along with all his letters; I was thrilled to have these words confessing his love for me in his own handwriting. Suddenly, I was sixteen again and reading love words from my husband, my love. I laughed and then I cried until late into the night when I finally fell asleep. So many memories were wrapped up in these precious things.

It wasn't long before the grief that I had stuffed way down inside me for all those years awakened once more and spilled out of me like a sleeping volcano erupting with full force. My heart ached as though the fifty years had vanished, and Dean had only just been killed. As the days passed, the grief became stronger. Many times, I found myself on my knees begging God to give him back to me. The tears I cried would fill an ocean. I sobbed and pleaded day after day and week after week to have him back. I had studied the Bible for many years and I know that God doesn't work that way. It didn't stop me from begging.

During the time this storm was going on inside of me, Houston experienced a huge storm that flooded much of the city. The church building flooded, including my office. Most everything was going to need to be reconstructed. I began working from home most days. I spent a lot of time alone and my grief escalated into a deep depression. I avoided everyone I knew, including my children. My fears grew, and my anger did, also. I was angry with everyone; at Dean for being killed as he tried to rescue a fellow soldier, at Sam for trying to take my memories away, at myself for not having enough love to keep Dean from dying and for not being strong enough to stand up to Sam. I was also angry with God for taking Dean away while I was praying continuously for his safety. I was so miserable and continued to have outbursts of anger which caused me more fear, more anger, and anxiety.

My therapist and I had assumed that the anger and fear I had experienced most of my adult life was the result of living with an alcoholic parent while growing up. We worked through that well. I don't know why, but we never talked about Dean in our sessions; only that I had been married twice. Though he never left my thoughts, it didn't occur to me that his death was related to the rage I felt inside me. But I was to discover that my anger and the terror I lived with were closely tied to the grief that I had tried to close my eyes to when I married Sam. When I thought back, I knew my acute anger began after Dean's death. As a child growing up with an alcoholic parent, I had never learned skills to deal with my problems. The pain had been so severe that I could not live with it, so I became the good girl and actress and acted the part I thought people expected of me. All the while I was just stuffing more and more hurt and anger inside myself.

So-called experts in grief counseling will tell you that there are five to seven phases of the grief process. I'm not sure what they would say about my experience, but I can tell you that in my case, not working through the steps early in my grief caused a sudden eruption or explosion of grief years after it should have been dealt with. This flare up, the feelings of anger, even hate, and sorrow can be directed towards one's self or others. In my case, it was both. I am a classic testimony to the truth that a huge avalanche of emotions can come from repressing grief for so many years.

I spent most of my time away from people. I read my Bible, trying to glean some comfort or answers from the God I had trusted for so many years. I literally prayed on my knees many times each day. I went to the cemetery almost every day to feel close to Dean. I had thought about Dean every day since the night we met; never was there a day when he did not come into my mind; not since I was thirteen. This is when I decided to have the ruby embedded into the wedding band Dean had given me and to wear it again. It gave me a bit of comfort. I had promised to be faithful to him and my guilt of being "unfaithful" when I married Sam was killing me.

Many times, I contemplated getting drunk or taking pills to dull the agonizing pain, even though I did not ever drink alcohol or take pills. I guess because it was the example I had learned as a child of how to handle problems. I knew from my growing up in an alcoholic environment that it only intensifies the problems. I contemplated suicide once again, which had been my solution many times in my life. But I had enough sense left in me that I couldn't hurt my family more.

I drowned myself in music. Mostly it was gospel songs. I had more than two hundred gospel songs on my playlist and listened to them every day. Then I discovered the music of Eric Clapton, which I had never even listened to before. I became obsessed with his life and career. During the 1970s, when he became popular, was during the time I hated all music after Dean was gone. And, as one of his songs says, I felt like I was *"drowning in a river of tears."* Another Clapton song explains exactly how I felt, *"It's like living in a nightmare…Like looking in the blackest hole…Like standing on the edge of nothing…Completely out of control."* He understood my pain because he had experienced it throughout his life.

I gained a lot of weight and kept my hair short after I married Sam. I didn't care how I looked. I wasn't trying to impress anyone. Suddenly, I started eating healthier than I had before and lost forty pounds in a short amount of time. I exercised like a maniac. I began to want to look good in my clothes and grow my hair a little longer. It had been many years since I cared about my appearance at all. It was like I was doing it for Dean, though I knew he wasn't here nor would he be. I seriously thought about having his name tattooed on my shoulder, though I have never liked tattoos.

I wrote a few songs and some poetry, which always before had been an outlet for my anger or frustration at having to lock up or deny my emotions? This time it didn't help much. I stopped my piano lessons. I had wanted to play since I was a small child. All the plans I had for making the house and landscape look nice were gone. Suddenly I had no interest in anything except my writing, my grandchildren, God, and Dean.

22. *Free At Last!*

My children surely thought that I had completely lost my mind. There were many times that I seriously questioned my sanity. I couldn't even have a conversation with them without bringing up the most recent discovery I had about this rock star's life. It was the only thing I knew to talk about, unless I told them how much I was suffering with my grief. I knew they did not want to hear that, nor would they understand it.

One Sunday morning I was listening to a favorite gospel song as I was driving to worship. The words were asking God for His healing touch. Tears began to roll down my face and I prayed again for God to heal me from my painful grief. I pleaded again for Him to give Dean back to me. Why couldn't I have the only thing I had ever wanted? What I wanted was Dean. He was all that I wanted. I wanted to go back to a time when he was with me and start over, though I knew it could not be. I was totally irrational.

Suddenly, I heard, not in my ears, but in my mind, *"My child, I have been giving him back to you for weeks, but you have not recognized it."* No, I didn't hear an audible voice in my ear, but it was very clear. I can't explain it, but I knew it was God talking to me. That is not the way I would speak. I do not call myself "my child." I pulled into a parking lot and stopped the car. As I sat there stunned at what I had "heard" I began to sob uncontrollably. Suddenly, I knew it was true; that God had given him back to me in the only way that He would. He had given me the freedom to speak Dean's name, the freedom to look at his pictures, to wear his ring, to visit his grave, to talk to people about my love for him. These things I had not been allowed to do for forty-nine years. I felt like a chain had been removed from my heart. I was finally free to profess my love for my beloved husband. *He had been given back to me!*

I guess I could have done those things for the last nineteen and a half years since Sam had been gone, but I had so trained myself to keep Dean and our life together, locked away inside me so there would be peace within our home. I also wasn't sure how my children would feel. I absorbed all the pain and harbored the anger and guilt inside my heart. My actions were typical of a child raised in a home with an alcoholic parent. It has taken me this long to break those chains.

I felt a joy in my heart that I had not felt for fifty years. I was excited and wanted to tell the people I loved most about this phenomenal transformation I was experiencing. Maybe I should have been prepared, but I did not expect the reaction I received from my children. They really did think I had lost my mind. They made it clear that they didn't like my music choices, my wearing Dean's ring, or my glowing joy. They didn't like that I was not the mother they had always known, though I don't know why they would want the angry and strict mom they had when they were children.

They accused me of loving Dean more than their dad; of being disloyal to their dad. There were other accusations, which were misinterpretations because they were seen through the eyes of children. Children cannot know all that goes on between their parents, but they can assume. Yes, I loved Dean first and more than anyone I have ever loved. But when I finally made a commitment to Sam and my children, I was a good and loyal wife to Sam for twenty-nine years. I wanted to tell them all the things their dad had done to keep me from loving him like he and they wanted me to, but I couldn't do that to them; they loved him.

Following their accusations, I had one of my fits of rage (another gift to children of alcoholic parents) and told them I would not be with them for Christmas which was a week away; and I wasn't. I spent Christmas Day in worship in the morning and reading a book alone in my house with a bowl of cereal for my Christmas dinner. It was my choice and though I missed my grandchildren, I had a quiet and peaceful day.

My heart was broken, but I could not give up this newfound freedom that God had given me. Why couldn't my children understand what I had been through all these years? It was because they didn't know the entire story. I could love Dean and their dad, the way a parent can love more than one child. Dean and Sam were totally different personalities. They had different interests, ideals, and goals. I loved Dean first and he was my life; he was the first person that I felt had really loved me un-conditionally. I had always been loyal to him. When other guys asked me out, I always said no; even to Sam. I know Sam felt that he was my second choice, but I didn't choose him at all. Looking back, I can see that many people I was close to pushed me towards a new relationship. I guess that my grief was a burden to them. They didn't know what to do with me or how to comfort me, so they were constantly urging me "move on."

Then Sam, himself, was pushing me and I didn't have the strength to keep resisting them all. I was weary of the fighting with my parents. I was vulnerable and so tired of the persistent pain. It was easier to just give in and stop the constant nagging; the advice coming from every side was too much for a sixteen or seventeen-year-old girl to endure.

When Sam died, I was never forced to deny my feelings for him or pretend he never existed. People around me weren't constantly trying to push me towards a new relationship. When he died, I could grieve for him and for the tremendous loss my children were feeling without inter-ference from my family and friends.

My children did not understand my feelings about Dean or that I had been manipulated into living a lie for many years. I'm sure Sam didn't set out to control my life; he wasn't a bad man. He loved me the way I loved Dean and wanted me to feel the same about him. Because of growing up in an alcoholic family with a lot of fighting, his anger made me afraid of him in the beginning of our marriage. Thus, I became the best wife I could be. I never denied him anything he wanted, whether it was food, softball, sex, golf, anything. In the beginning, I rarely gave an opinion about what I wanted to do. We were married several years before I realized I didn't have to fear him; he wasn't violent.

I knew that I couldn't keep living in the fantasy world I had been living in for so long. If that meant I would lose my family, so be it. I had been molded into the person Sam wanted me to be; I didn't even recognize myself after a while. I had continued the charade for nineteen years after he died because it was what everyone was comfortable with. Until I was faced with another choice; a choice of freedom. It was unfair to expect me to continue living that sham and remain in an angry state of mind for the rest of my life. God had given me this gift of freedom. How could I refuse Him when I had asked for His help and He answered me?

As a Christian, I was determined to allow God to guide me in the direction He chose. I pleaded with God to heal me. I wanted to be the person I was before I developed all the anger I was feeling. I constantly prayed that I was not misinterpreting His answers. Though I was not always sure my choices were where He was leading me, He never redirected me in this at all. I regard that as being His will.

23. Revelations To Peace

IT WAS TIME TO GET SERIOUS ABOUT GETTING SOME DIRECTION and peace in my life. I needed to begin healing, but I didn't know where to start. After almost a year, my office was ready to move back into. I was so glad to have an opportunity to be with people again. One thing I learned from my therapist, was that I needed to talk about my life with people I trusted and not keep my feelings bottled up. People living in an alcohol or substance abusive home do not tell anyone about what goes on at home. It stays inside them. So, in my heartache, as the opportunity presented itself, I talked to my friends about my grief. Most of them knew Sam from church, but I told them about Dean; some of them didn't even know I had been married before Sam. I was afraid that they would not approve of what I told them. Many of them loved Sam. I was wrong. They loved me also and encouraged me to continue my trek to a healthy future.

I woke up each morning with Dean on my mind. I went to sleep at night with Dean on my mind. He dominated my thoughts during the day and my dreams at night. It kept going through my mind, "Dean will always be nineteen and I am in my sixties. When he was killed, he was the age my oldest grandson is now. He would have been sixty-nine this year. I prayed every day for God to show me the way to heal from my grief and bring peace to my life. He has never let me down.

I had no idea how or when God would answer my prayer, but I had faith in His way and His timing. I continued my time with God every morning, studying His Word, talking with Him, and sitting quietly in meditation as I had done for many years. I humbled myself by praying on my knees, and even sobbing and begging for His help. When I prayed, the anguish I felt in my heart eased a bit so that I could function during my day, but it would soon return. The tears would start without warning wherever I was. It was sometimes embarrassing to me. I asked God, *"Lord, when will I ever stop crying over losing him? I know You are healing me, but it's taking so long. I am so tired of crying."* Little did I know that my healing journey had just begun and what a long and painful journey it would be. I am not superstitious, nor do I believe in luck or coincidence, but soon some very unusual things started happening in my life.

About once a year or so, I look at my old high school alumni website at the list of students I graduated with to see if there is news about anyone or if anyone has died that I knew back then. One lazy evening, I checked the website as I was finished talking with friends on Facebook. Dean had gone to the same school ahead of me, so I usually looked at his class, since many of his friends became my friends, also. Students can leave notes to one another or make comments about their friends there. When I checked Dean's name, there was a pretty long note someone had written there. It was from Cecil, one of his friends that he grew up with and went to school and church with. They had been in Basic Training at Fort Polk, LA together and in Vietnam at the same time. I had met him only a couple of times when we double dated, but I recognized his name and remembered that he was in one or two of the pictures from Fort Polk Dean had given me before he left for Vietnam.

The message had information about Dean's growing up years that I didn't know. He had written a note also about being in the same hospital in Japan that Dean had been in, but after Dean had been sent back to his unit. He accidently learned of Dean being in that hospital because he saw his name on a registration page when he was signing it. I was so happy to see it. Though I had searched for him once before and not found him, I looked his name up again on Facebook and there he was. I sent him a private message, "Are you the Cecil who was friends with Dean Whitlock?" He confirmed, "Yes, are you the BJ that was married to him?"

We messaged back and forth several times and talked about getting together for coffee the next week and talking about Dean. He said he had some funny stories about Dean he wanted to share with me and I was going to share my pictures with him. Circumstances prevented us from meeting, but after a few weeks he messaged me that he would call me to have lunch the next week. I was sad when he didn't contact me again, but it was a connection with Dean that I had not had before. I'm sure God's hand guided me to that web site that night and then stumbling onto that note. He had begun the healing process in me, though I didn't realize it yet.

One evening, as I was looking online to get some new books for my Kindle, I came across a book written by John Steinbeck about his self-appointed correspondent adventure in Vietnam. He was one of my favorite authors and I studied his style of writing when I wrote, so of course it caught my attention. The husband of his former editor, who had passed away, had agreed to receive the articles from Steinbeck, written as letters to his editor as if she was still living. This man who was the publisher of the daily newspaper, *Newsday*, also agreed to print these letters in his paper. In these writings, he chronicled his experiences in Vietnam from December 1966 to April 1967.

Dean was there in December of 1966 and killed on January 10 of 1967. I had never heard about Steinbeck going to Vietnam and I was curious. I immediately purchased the book for my Kindle and soon I ordered a hard copy, also. I had always loved his work, but I was about to become personally connected to him. I like his sarcastic sense of humor. His writings always bring to life whatever he is writing about. You can see very clearly whatever he is describing; his description of the HUEY pilots he rode with in Vietnam is a beautiful picture of pure genius. He compares them to *"controlling a fine, well-trained quarter horse; weaving along stream beds; they rise like swallows to clear trees; like sure and seemingly slow hands of Pablo Casals on the cello; like musician's hands they play their controls like music and dance them like ballerinas."*

The purpose of his undertaking was to get a more personal perspective of the war from the soldiers and the South Vietnamese people. His younger son, John, was stationed in Saigon and his older son was in the States, about to be deployed. He wanted to see firsthand what this war was like. He had reported from the World War II battlefields and had a keen interest in the military and in this current war. He felt a need to see if the protests of this war, going on in the States, were justified. He concluded that they were not. I read of some of the atrocities he wrote about that the enemy had committed against our soldiers and their own people. Steinbeck witnessed the results of this horror himself.

A Marine major was assigned to him as a guide. He flew on missions with the men on the Huey helicopters, he learned to fire their M-60 machine gun and their M-16 automatic rifle, and he went on watch with a Navy captain on the patrol boats in the Mekong Delta. There were several missions that he was given permission to go along on and many other weapons he was allowed to fire. He knew and understood weapons, operations, and war. He truly had an up close and personal view of what was happening in Vietnam.

As I was reading, I saw that he also traveled with General William Westmoreland to visit the farthest outpost near the Cambodian border. They spent Christmas Day 1966 with the 101st Airborne in Kontum Province, Vietnam meeting soldiers and taking pictures. It was thirteen days before Dean was killed in Kontum Province. I realized that Dean was there on that Christmas Day. I remembered a couple of the pictures that I received from Dean just before he was killed were of General Westmoreland with some soldiers. I went immediately to the case where

I kept Dean's pictures and sure enough, John Steinbeck was in the background behind General Westmoreland who was about to greet Dean with a handshake.

I would not have known that if I had not come across the Steinbeck book. Coincidence? I don't think so. Dean knew I loved John Steinbeck writings. He would have told me about that encounter if he had come home. I found the pictures when the time was right for me. Remember, I had asked God to heal me from my painful grieving?

It is very interesting to me how the reading of Steinbeck's book has set my mind to whirling and imaging pictures in my head. He writes in such detail and describes with such an array of vivid words to draw that I can almost hear the ear-piercing blasts as the bombs find their targets; hear the laughter of the soldiers as they tried to forget why they were there, if only for a while; hear the choppy sound of the rotors on the HUEYS overhead; and hear the monkeys in the trees without seeing them. I can feel the fear in the gut of these heroic men; feel the slimy mud they have caked on their boots and fatigues; and feel the never-ending rain on their heads and their backs, the leeches and biting bugs on their skin, and feel the heat they must endure when the rain stops.

I can taste the C-rations, the putrid water, the beer, and the occasional treat sent from home. I can smell the gun powder; the rotting filth, the burning flesh, and the death all around them. I can dream the dreams of the soldiers as they think of a sweet mother, a worried dad, a child, a wife or lover back home.

I began to have dreams about my Dean as he lived this life of a warrior before he was killed. In my dreams, I can see him quietly walking through the elephant grass in the rain, when suddenly gunfire! His friend ahead of him is hit and Dean runs to help him. Too late, the sniper gets him also. As he lies there dying in that God forsaken place, he remembers my face and our love as he slips away.

I have had dreams of him returning to me. I see him stepping off the plane and me not being able to make my legs run fast enough to reach him. Our arms tighten around one another as if they will never be loosed again. In one of the dreams we were at home. He was bathing in a large tub and I was scrubbing the mud off him that somehow had made it home with him from the rice paddies. He grabbed me and pulled me into the tub with him, kissing me and holding me like he would never let me go. These dreams leave me shaken when I wake up, sometimes crying before I am even fully awake, and I am very sad for the day or days ahead.

The vivid descriptions in this book made me hungry to know more about the world Dean lived in without me. We had been together for two and a half years and I knew all about him in that time as well as the little his mother and grandmother had told me about his childhood, but the seven months he was in Vietnam I knew very little about. I began to do research on the war, particularly the 101st Airborne Division. I found military operations he was in or could have been a part of, like Operation Seward where he was likely wounded and sent to the hospital in Japan. Also, Operation Pickett where he received his fatal wound.

There were reports written about these Search and Destroy missions and the missions to protect rice paddies for the South Vietnamese people. I also learned that the 101st Airborne unit he was with had the nickname of *"First Strike."* God led me to some amazing information that gave me a picture of his time there. It's like piecing a puzzle together of that seven-month period that has been blank for me. One puzzle piece led me to another one and another. I am finally seeing a part of the picture of his day to day life during those months and it's hard to look at sometimes.

24. Blasted From The Past

ONE OF MY FRIENDS DIED DURING THE TIME I WAS READING Steinbeck's book. She was buried directly across the pond from Dean's grave. I don't think that was an accident. One cool Sunday afternoon as I was driving home from worship service, I decided to drive by and see the new grave marker her daughter had told me was installed the day before. Naturally, I wanted to visit with Dean while I was there. As I was walking towards my car from Dean's grave, a woman and her husband were getting out of their car next to mine. She said, "Excuse me, I don't mean to bother you, but are you a relative of this young man." She pointed to Dean's marker.

"Yes, I was his wife," I answered.

"I remember when he was killed," she continued. "I worked at Welex, where he worked before he went into the Army. I was the one who collected money from the other workers to buy flowers for his funeral. I didn't really know him, but I knew of him. My parents are buried just a few steps away from him. I've never met any of his family and I just wanted to say how sorry I am. I have wondered about his family and prayed for you all each time I come here."

I was stunned and reaching back into my memory. My mother had worked at the place she mentioned, but she didn't remember my mother. Suddenly, I had a slight memory of Mother getting Dean a job there. I had not thought of that in many years. He had only worked there for a

119

few months when he enlisted in the Army. I thanked her for taking the trouble to tell me about that and I gave her, this complete stranger, a hug. Why was she there on that Sunday, at the exact time that I was there? Coincidence? Not a chance.

I called my mother when I got to my car and asked her if she knew the woman and if she remembered Dean working there. She said she didn't know the woman but did remember helping him get a job there; that she and Dean had shared a ride to work together. She had not thought about it in a long time until I asked her.

Most of the people that knew Dean and me, I have lost contact with or they have passed on, also. I had lost contact with my friend, Becky, who had moved out of state when we were in school just before I met Dean. She and her husband had moved back to Houston for a few years after Sam and I married and then went back to Mississippi. We had not talked in years. Suddenly, one day, she sent a message through Facebook. We talked for a while and she asked me, "Do you ever wonder how things would be if Dean had come home?"

I answered her, "Every day for fifty years." Finally, I had someone that remembered him that I could talk with about him. We have continued to message back and forth, sometimes about old times or about Dean, but also about our grandchildren. Was her timing an accident a coincidence, just when I needed to talk to someone who knew him? No way.

25. God's Perfect Plan

ONE EVENING, MY FRIEND, CONNIE, AND I WENT TO DINNER. SHE has always encouraged me to write and been a positive influence in my life. She started asking questions about how I was doing. She knew how I had been grieving. She suggested that I join a support group for people who had lost a loved one in the Vietnam War. Since I am such a shy and private person, I told her that I really didn't want to do that, besides I didn't have a clue as to how I could find such a group since the war was so long ago.

"I have contacts that could help find out about them," she offered. Connie worked for a local television station and did know people. She told me to let her know if I changed my mind and she still encouraged me to continue my writing. I confided in her about my obsession with the rock singer and let her see some song lyrics I had written. We talked about my recent loneliness without my children. Then we promised to meet again soon for dinner and we went home.

About a month later, I received information on Facebook from a Vietnam Veterans' group. They said members shared original pictures from their time in Vietnam; pictures of their friends who were killed in the war, and an assortment of pictures taken during the Vietnam War. I have always searched each face I see in the news, books, movies, and magazines to see if Dean is there. I don't even think about it, I just do it. I've been doing it since the day he landed in Vietnam. This would be an opportunity to see pictures from people who were actually there. The administrators of this particular group had to give permission for the members to join and had rules about no politics or disrespectful posts about any other members.

I sent a message requesting membership. I told them that I was a widow of a soldier killed in action in Vietnam fifty years ago. The message I received back said, "You definitely belong here." In the first two hours after I was accepted, I received four hundred and fifty hits with sympathy for me and honor for Dean, welcoming me, or some words of encouragement. Well, I had found a support group like Connie had suggested. Was this another coincident or God at work in my life?

Through this support group I have read many comments and conversations from Vietnam Veterans. They have relayed the terrible conditions they lived with daily and the battles and the uncertain fear of their next move. I have been introduced to hundreds of pictures of their life there and videos of the men and women, the country, and even the fighting. It was horrifying to know that Dean experienced these things in his last months. These men have a variety of attitudes about the war that range from deep religious faith to tremendous hate for government officials that made decisions about the war. The veterans in this group have been beneficial to my healing expedition in their comments of comfort and pride in Dean's sacrifice.

One Saturday afternoon I received a message from Cecil. I had not heard from him in three months and assumed he wasn't interested in connecting with an old acquaintance. "I apologize for taking so long to contact you", he said, "but I had to "get my head together" before I could see you." It didn't occur to me that seeing me would bring back memories of Vietnam or that he felt guilty about him returning and Dean not coming home to me. Cecil had no wife and Dean had me waiting for him. He said that he had thought of me many times and wondered how I was doing. Dean's mother went to Cecil's wedding and she told him I was not doing well. I had read several comments from other veterans in my support group that had those same *survivor's guilt* feelings.

Cecil, his wife, and I met for lunch one day; we talked. He told me that just after he had seen Dean's name on the register in the hospital, he received a letter from an old friend that he and Dean had known in high school. She told him about Dean's death. I could tell it was hard for him to talk about Dean. I shared pictures with him and gave him a copy of John Steinbeck's book. We haven't talked since, but I hope our visit helped him as much as it did me. This was no accident; God's timing is always perfect.

During the time of my connection with the support group, my younger sister came from Tennessee to visit. She was twelve when Dean was killed, but she naturally remembered him and even had a crush on him when he and I were dating. I know God sent her to me at a time when I was ready to talk about the details of my grief that I couldn't share with anyone else. She listened, and we cried together like real sisters as I lay my burden at her feet. I had always thought of her as my child because I took care of her when we were growing up. She was such a comfort to me and encouraged me to continue to heal. Her visit was an unplanned, last minute decision. I'm sure God sent her to me at the right time.

26. Getting Real Is Painful

Military videos

Following my sister's visit, I was introduced, by one of the veterans in the group, to some military videos of the 101st Airborne Division and their operations in the war. Specifically, the videos were of CO B, 2D BN, 502 INF, 1st BDE 101st Airborne Division, in November 1966 to January 31, 1967. This was Dean's unit and he was KIA on January 10, 1967. It was during Operation Pickett at Kontum Province, Vietnam near the Cambodian border. I had read a previously confidential document that gave details of this operation with objectives, statistics, and what they learned from it, but this was video. I searched in vain for Dean's face. It was very emotional for me to watch. My heart was pounding as I watched the soldiers with their weapons blazing, but I could not take my eyes away from it. I didn't even know these videos existed, but this was the time God had planned for me to see them. I will continue to search videos, pictures, and information about the last months of his life of which I was a part of only through my letters of love and his thoughts and dreams of me.

Jamie

From time to time, I look for old friends on Facebook, just out of curiosity. Most of the time they aren't there. Then sometimes I find one, as I did when I found Cecil, after years of checking and not finding them before. I decided to look for Dean's friend Jamie, that became my friend also. He is the blond guy, Jamie, that was with Dean the night we met. The last I had heard anything about him was when Dean's mother told me that he had returned from Vietnam and sometime later married. She also told me that he and his wife had a baby that died. I wasn't allowed to contact him at the time to offer my condolences. I had searched for him a couple of times since last year when my grief started, but with no results.

The next time Connie and I went to dinner, she asked about my "healing journey" as we called it. I had told her about Jamie in earlier conversations, and said, "Connie, he has been on my mind so much lately. I really want to talk to him, but I don't know where he is." I had also told her about Sheila, the girl he had dated that held me up as I went into the funeral home to see Dean's body for the first time. We all lost touch a long time ago.

"Don't give up," she told me, "you don't know what God's plan is." That was the end of the conversation. We talked about my writings and her annual project at work that took her to Washington D.C., then we said good night.

It was late when I got home, about 11:30. I went through my routine bedtime activities, slipped into my pajamas, into bed, and turned out the light. I was almost asleep when I received a message notification on my phone. I looked at the time; it was 12:02 a.m. When I checked it, I had to gasp. It was from Sheila, Jamie's old girlfriend. We had not spoken in fifty years. She wanted to become friends on Facebook! She told me all about her kids and grandkids, her retirement, and her husband. I didn't say much because I was in shock. Between our messages to one another I sent a text to Connie to tell her what was happening. I was freaking out a little. Connie reminded me that God is in control, to relax and let Him work. Sheila asked if I ever saw Dean's brother, who was also friends with

Jamie. I told her that we had not talked for a very long time. Then the messages stopped.

By the next morning, I felt a strong need to talk with Jamie, so I searched for him again on Facebook and found him. It brought back so many memories when I saw his face. There was a picture of him in his Army uniform. I wondered what he looked like now. I remembered the night I met him and Dean, the night we talked with him before Dean took me to meet his parents, all of us listening to records at his and Dean's apartment, double dating with him and his girl, and Dean's funeral when I went to him and hugged him before entering the limo for the drive to the cemetery. I looked through my pictures and located pictures of Jamie and me at my house in the days following the funeral. I really did want to talk to him, but I didn't send a personal message this time for fear it would disturb him as it had Cecil. Jamie had gone to Vietnam shortly after Dean's funeral.

As I continued to search, I came across Jamie's son who, I was surprised to learn, lives about seven miles from me. Then I read on his son's Facebook page that Jamie had passed away six months before. He is buried in the same cemetery where Dean is. It broke my heart. He had been a good friend to Dean and to me and I truly wanted to talk to him. I contacted his son and explained who I was. He told me that several times his dad, when they were visiting family graves there, had taken him by Dean's grave and told him that Dean was his best friend who had died in Vietnam. He wants to meet with me and share stories about these two precious friends. I would love to tell him how his dad would go with Dean and I sometimes and I would sit between the two of them in the front seat. One day Dean said to Jamie, "Look man, you're gonna have to get your own girl. I'm not sharing mine with you." I remember how Jamie's face turned red. Whether Jamie's son and I meet in person or not, I know God allowed me to find him, so I could know about Jamie's passing.

Surprisingly, I have cried and mourned for Jamie even after all these years. We were friends and remembering him brings memories of Dean. These memories have made me very sad, but I am looking forward to meeting his son if it works out. Coincidence? I don't believe in them. God is healing me in ways that I cannot comprehend, yet, but I continue to wait and watch for His guidance. I have not heard from Sheila again. I suspect she wanted to get in touch with Jamie through Dean's brother.

One day, about six months later while leaving the cemetery, I saw some marble or granite headstones lining a sidewalk and leading to a large open Bible with the Lord's Prayer on it. For some reason, I stopped to look at this place I had not noticed before. There was a cement bench next to a tree. There was a breeze and I decided to sit for a while before getting back in the car. As I sat, I turned to look at some of the markers nearby. I could not believe my eyes. There about four feet from me was Jamie's grave and marker. I had looked for it a couple of times, but the cemetery is so large that it was an impossible task. I don't know why I accidently found where his grave is, but if I need to know, God will let me know. I did leave a yellow friendship rose on his grave the next time I was there.

Love confirmed

Through the years, I have become so insecure about Dean's love for me; because I didn't have any of his letters and had been told he didn't love me my doubts grew. I had been told so many things that I wasn't sure were true or not and it had been so many years. Even though I had the love notes on the back of his pictures, I wondered if I was remembering it the way I wanted it to be or the way I had been told by those who had their own agendas. I began to pray for God to please send me confirmation of Dean's love; something that I could not deny. I had hoped that

Jamie would confirm it for me, but since he was gone I could think of no one, still living, to validate it for me. All I could do was hope God would bless me in a way that only He could see.

One Saturday morning in June, I was at home waiting for the air conditioner repair man to come repair my unit. The house was hot, and I had been waiting since the evening before to get the house cool again. It can make one a little irritable to say the least. I received a notification on my Messenger that someone was contacting me. I have some great Facebook friends; we pray together, laugh together, share information, and encourage one another daily. I assumed it was one of them reaching out to me about something. It was not. It was my cousin, Tessa. She is the one who is married to Sam's brother. Dean and I would hang out with them regularly in the last few months we were dating. Dean was learning to play the guitar from her husband. I had been distanced from her for many years. Since she and her husband knew Dean and me when we were together, I had been strongly discouraged from seeing her. I opened the message and there staring back at me was one of my favorite pictures of Dean; no one other than I had a copy of that picture. He sent it to me just before he was killed. Where did she get it; it belonged to me. She asked if I had seen it, that it was on a Vietnam Wall page. I told her, "Yes, it's my picture; I put it on the page." We talked for several minutes about incidents that had happened over the years and how Sam had tried to keep me from contacting people who reminded me of Dean. She heard from my mother that I wanted to go see the Vietnam Memorial Wall. I received encouragement from her to go to Washington D.C. The visit with her turned out to be nice, though at first, I was very uncomfortable. I explained how angry I had been for so many years and why. She mentioned that she remembered how much I loved Dean and how he adored me. I was sure she was just saying what she thought I would want her to say.

During the week, I thought a lot about my talk with Tessa on

Messenger. I wanted to apologize for being so distant and unfriendly with her and her family for so long. Finally, I decided to contact her and ask if we could meet to talk. I didn't realize that she had moved too far away to get together on short notice, but she gave me her phone number to call her on Saturday morning. I was nervous about actually talking with her, so I talked to God about it and asked for courage and guidance. It turned out to be such a good phone visit and a blessing. We caught up on our families and talked about grandchildren, of course.

As we talked, the conversation turned to old times and the times Dean and I spent with them. She told me that she had never known a couple so much in love as Dean and I were. She said over and over how she remembered the way Dean looked at me; that anyone could tell he was in love with me. I started to cry, and she was confused until I told her about my prayer. Then Tessa said, "I can see why you would have doubts after all this time without his letters that declared his love. I remember that you even read parts of some of his letters to me where he told you how much he loved and missed you. I remember you waiting every day for the mail to come. But you have to know that everyone knew how much he loved you." This conversation was exactly what I needed to alleviate my doubts about Dean's love, from someone who had been there with us. Had God answered my prayer? Absolutely! No coincidence here. With each incident that I have described I felt a little healing of my heart. I catch myself listening for God and watching for what He will do next.

27. Amazing, Healing Wall

IT HAS NEVER BEEN EASY FOR ME TO TRAVEL. IT HAS BEEN ONE OF my fears, but I have decided that I do want to go to Washington D.C. to visit the Vietnam Memorial Wall. I have received encouragement from many in the support group, Tessa, and my friend, Connie as well as several other friends. They say it could be a healing experience and that I should go. Now, I am waiting for confirmation from God that He is in favor of this trip. I know, of course, that Dean's name is on the Wall; his mother went to see it before she passed away. I just couldn't see how looking at his name on a Wall could heal me. After all, I had looked at his name on his grave marker hundreds of times and only feel sad and lonely. Another friend went to the Wall with her husband a few years ago and brought me a rubbing of Dean's name from the Wall. I know the location of his name; it is panel E14 line 8.

A trip like this would be expensive and I needed a traveling companion, but I went to God with the request for His blessing. After some weeks of prayer, God made it possible for me to go. I received a financial reward that was unexpected. I was blessed by having my oldest grandson, Boomer, agree to travel with me. I'm not sure how it happened, but God always comes through for me with an answer. It isn't always yes, and the answer isn't always clear at first, but He lets me know in His eternal way what I need to do.

Many people would say that these incidents were just happenstance, a fluke of some sort, but I believe God has been answering my prayers in this way so that I can heal from the grief that I have carried around for fifty years. Otherwise, why haven't these *accidents* occurred before now?

Tears at the Wall

The trip to Washington D.C. was the first time for Boomer to fly and only the second for me. He was a little apprehensive until we were in the air. Now he wants to travel no other way. My adult grandson was the perfect companion for me on this venture. He understood the Metro and the trains more quickly than I could have figured out. We stayed in the Foggy Bottom district which is near George Washington University so there were college students everywhere. It is also one of the older parts of the city and not far from the Vietnam Memorial Wall. We decided to go the second day after we arrived to visit the Monuments and Memorials.

Washington D.C. was not what I expected it to be at all. I had studied the map and knew the area where the Wall was located, near the Lincoln Memorial and the Reflecting Pool. I chose the hotel I thought would be the closest to that site. I planned some other activities to do with my grandson, including a train trip to Baltimore to watch the Orioles and Astros baseball game; we both are avid Astros fans. We arrived on Thursday afternoon, checked into the hotel, took a walk to familiarize ourselves with the area, went to dinner, and back to the hotel.

Early Friday morning we got ready and went to breakfast in the hotel restaurant. Then we began our seven-block trek to the memorials. Washington D.C. blocks are much longer than the ones we have at home. I was tired when we arrived; partly because of the walk and more because of my anxiety over our mission. We saw the Lincoln Memorial, the Washington Monument, and the World War II, and Korean Memorials. Soon we located the Vietnam Memorial Wall. My tears started to flow as soon as I saw the beautiful, black granite structure; it was massive and filled with fifty-eight thousand three hundred seven names.

These are the number of families and friends who have a hole in their heart where their missing loved one once lived. Each of these families have experienced the pain of waiting and praying for their loved one; the horror of hearing the news that he or she was not coming home alive; of planning a funeral instead of a homecoming celebration; of learning to wake up each morning and put one foot in front of the other to get through each day knowing it will be without the one they love. I was not alone in these heartaches. I think that is what makes this a healing experience. That is what the veterans have told me.

The "Wall" was much longer than I realized. The dignity of it with so many names was overwhelming, to say the least. My legs felt like Jell-o and when we found the correct panel, I could not make myself look for his name for a few minutes. It was the same feeling I had when I went to the funeral home to view his body on the first day he was returned from Vietnam. I held back not wanting it to be real. When I finally made myself look up at his name, the tears flowed freely. I hate to cry in front of strangers, but when I saw his name, everyone around me disappeared and it was just Dean and me, like that day so many years before when I saw him in that red Chevy next to my school bus.

It was comforting to have Boomer near me. I became conscious of the fact, as I stood there looking at Dean's name, that Boomer is six months older than Dean was when he was killed. Time marches on whether we are ready or not. We had planned to grow old together and have children and grandchildren; instead I am old with children and grandchildren and he is still nineteen. It's a hard reality for me.

I located the name of one of Dean's brothers-in-arms that was killed June 10, 1967, exactly five months after Dean. I am now trying to locate some of his family members to share some pictures of him that Dean sent to me. Maybe this will be another healing step, for those who have names on the Wall, to help one another. We are a community of survivors, a family, if you will. Encouraging one another could be a key in our healing process. It couldn't hurt.

As I stood with the black granite looming above me, Boomer walked away to give me some private time with Dean. I placed an "air-mail" envelope filled with a note from me, a picture of us together, and a newspaper clipping with his picture from when he was killed, in front of the panel where his name is engraved. Then I stood back and looked up at his name for several minutes, tears falling all the time. It was such an emotional, but epic experience. I will always treasure my first visit to the "Wall."

Later in the day, Boomer showed me some pictures he took of me that I was not aware of. Two were of me standing back looking up at Dean's name as my tears streamed down my face.

The third picture was of me placing the envelope in front of the panel; as I bent over to place the envelope, my image was reflected in the black granite of the Wall making a double image. The picture is a little blurry, but maybe that is as it should be. It was an amazing shot. We stayed in D.C. for four days and I wanted to go back to the Wall one more time, but time and exhaustion on my part prevented it.

We were there two more days and saw many things. Brendan was impressed with the fact that much of the historical events we viewed in the museums had occurred in my lifetime. I filled him in on my memories of each one. I think he gained a new respect for and an interest in his country's history.

I did not have an opportunity to return to the Wall. I hope to go again one day soon. I would recommend anyone who is searching for peace from the grief they are still experiencing after so many painful years following this terrible war, go to the "Wall." Take God with you there and touch the stone, make a rubbing of the name, talk to other family members who are there; maybe it will ease your pain to some extent.

Unexpected Revelations

In the weeks after we returned home, God revealed so many lessons I needed to learn. It had to be from the journey to witness the "Wall." One lesson I learned is to trust God completely in His plan. It is always perfect, and I can never have a better way of doing it. He is the Creator. Who better to plan what comes next in my life? He has become my greatest desire since the trip. Dean has always been my greatest desire until now. Our love, as wonderful as it was and is, can never measure up to the love God has for me or the reward He has waiting for me in eternity. Wow! I can't even imagine anything better than the love Dean and I had. Jesus promised that it will be glorious.

Another lesson learned was forgiveness. Though I have known in the back of my mind why Sam tried to destroy my love for Dean, I wanted to stay angry at him. I thought I needed someone to blame for my pain. Sam loved me as much as I loved Dean. He wanted me to love him the same way and in his young and jealous mind he determined that if there were no physical reminders of Dean's existence, I would transfer my love to him. I understand why he did what he did. I know his life growing up was not the loving home a child should have. Growing up poor with seven siblings and an absentee dad could not have prepared him for making good choices or how to deal with marriage relationship. It was only when he matured, and we developed our own relationship with one another and with God that he understood that what he had done was to cement Dean in my mind and my heart even more. That is when he asked for my forgiveness.

Dean will always be my first, young, passionate, perfect love. I will always love and miss him. But as Sam and I lived together with our children and faced trials and joy, I learned to love him in a different way. It was a love brought together by our love for our family and for God. Because of the way our marriage started, it was not always easy or without difficulties, but I am grateful for the godly husband and father he became.

One of my friends recently posted the following on Facebook:

I had my own notion of grief.
I thought it was the sad time
That followed the death of someone you love.
And that you had to push through it to get to the other side.
But I'm learning that there is no other side,
There is no pushing through
But rather there is absorption,
Adjustment, and

Acceptance
Grief is not something that you complete,
But rather you endure.
Grief is not a task to finish and move on,
But an element of yourself,
An alteration of your being,
A new way of seeing,
A new definition of self.

I wish someone had clarified grief this way to me a long time ago. It makes so much sense in my mind; it is a perfect explanation. All these years I've been waiting to get past my grief and now I know I never will...It's not meant to be done that way.

28. Sunshine Of Forgiveness

THIS UNDERTAKING HAS BEEN THERAPEUTIC FOR ME AS I WAS DE-
prived of living through my grief for many years. This book was written
with many tears of sadness, frustration, and yes, even anger, for the strug-
gles and heartache I suffered because I fell in love and lost him in a way
I will never understand. I know that I will always love him, miss him,
and grieve for him.

I realize that my friends and family do not understand my grief after
such a long time. Another Clapton song, *"What words do I use to try to
explain to those who've witnessed all my tears."* The guilt I have felt for my
bad choices has been overwhelming at times. My life has been defined by
fear and much anger since losing Dean. It touched everyone around me
even if they didn't know where it was coming from. I do feel that I have
broken out of the shell that I had around me for so many years. I finally
feel more like myself again, but older and hopefully wiser. Most people I
know today, have never known the real me, not even my children.

So, have I forgiven Sam for his actions brought on by his jealousy of
Dean? I hope that this venture has brought me closer to forgiving Sam.
Most of the time I feel like I have forgiven him, but there are times when
I remember the things he did to remove Dean from my mind, and it still
hurts. I hope that doesn't mean I have not forgiven him. I talk to God every day about this. I have asked Him to teach me to forgive myself also,
as He forgives me each day.

The Vietnam War Family

I am only one of the emotionally wounded survivors of, not only the Vietnam War, but all wars. Thousands of families have their own stories of battling their personal grief and loneliness that any war brings. I have read many of their stories and they sound so heartbreakingly familiar.

The veterans who returned from Vietnam as heroes were mistreated by the Americans they had fought for. Their wives, parents, children, and friends were often ignored by our countrymen in our pain. Many of these returning warriors have died still wondering, "why?" A lot of them have died from horrible diseases caused by the chemicals they were exposed to in Vietnam. So many have died at their own hands because they could not heal from their emotional and physical pain. They have had to battle the government for their military benefits, including the healthcare they needed and deserved.

I have also read first-hand accounts of the atrocities executed on captured Americans and their own people by the Viet Cong. Our men witnessed these and viewed their brothers-in-arms killed before their eyes, sometimes in horrendous ways, knowing the next one to fall might be them. They experienced all this while serving their time in Vietnam for their country. No human should have the memories these veterans have. I read the following quote in an article about the young men. They developed their own ways of coping with what they saw. When they were *"hot, dirty with an ageless dirt, tired beyond physical endurance, weary to the bone, scared, skeptical of authority that had lied to them too many times before, boys who had done more than they could in good conscience do, seen more than they could bear to see, lost more than they could afford to lose, when conditions seemed impossibly unbearable, uttered these painful words that became a common saying among the vets, 'It don't mean nothin' also 'Ain't no big thing'."* I still hear them say it today as they talk about their experiences there. I've seen pictures of some who had what they called the *"thousand-yard stare.*" It is a haunting facial expression after they have witnessed many unimaginable sights; things no human should ever have to see. I have one picture of Dean with the beginnings of that haunting look in his eyes. It breaks my heart.

It is harder for me to forgive the politicians and governments who sent our young boys to be slaughtered in that tiny country. An entire generation of very young men, eighteen to twenty-one years old, were either killed, damaged by the horrors there, or are dying a slow death from the poison they breathed and ate, sprayed by our own people on the jungle where they were fighting. The politicians went home to their families each night and felt safe because the ones they put in jeopardy were protecting them. Hopefully, in time, the bitterness many of us feel about this will fade.

Our generation of men had been brought up on World War II movies with John Wayne and Lee Marvin heroes; they had strategic battle plans executed to wage the war and win it. Vietnam was not like that at all. It was chaos, horror, and evil that is unimaginable to people who have not been there. There was no strategy, no definite plan of action, just killing and torturing of innocent and brave people by the NVA.

29. *Flood Of Blessings*

ABOUT NINE DAYS AFTER I THOUGHT I WAS FINISHED WITH THIS
book, there was a storm in my area of Texas. Hurricane Harvey hit with
power and determination. I had been through several of these storms
and my house had never flooded in all the years since my parents built it
thirty years ago. I wasn't concerned, but cautious. Not only did Harvey
hit us and move inland as far as Austin, but he turned around and gave
us another pounding and stuck around for a while. Yes, my house flooded. There was three feet of water in my house. It took three days for the
water to recede to a point that I could drive my car across the bridge and
through the streets to my house. I lost almost everything I had accumu-
lated in the past fifty years.

Most of my pictures were stored on a shelf six feet off the floor and
were saved. But the first thing I saw when I opened the door was that
there was about an inch of water on the floor and my album, that I had
just filled with Dean's pictures, was lying in the dirty water. The book was
stuck in the mud that had collected on the floor and was soaked through.
I cried out and began to weep. Thankfully I had scanned all the pictures
into my computer and saved them on an external hard drive. I had even
scanned the love notes. My computer was destroyed by the flood and
could not be saved, but I still had the external drive.

I was staying with my mother at my aunt's house. One evening my
cousin, Darlene, helped me dislodge the pictures from the album. We

talked like we had never done. She was a young child when Dean and I were dating. She had a fond memory of him teaching her to wink her eyes, one at a time. Cute. Most of the pictures had been protected by the plastic page covers, but the writing on the back was gone. The weather was sweltering, but it provided a good environment for drying the photographs. We placed them on a towel inside my car. It took two or three days until they could be removed and stored. A few months later I took the most damaged ones and had them professionally restored. The other items that I had saved, our marriage license, a 101st Airborne flag, and all my treasured mementos were also salvaged as they were on a high bookshelf in the briefcase where I kept them.

With the help of my children and their families, along with many friends, we began the tortuous task of removing the wet items from my house and into the yard. I lost all my rugs, furniture, books, bedding, appliances, most of my clothes and shoes, and much more. Then we had to cut out five feet of the drywall, which wasn't dry any longer, from the walls in every room. It was an unpleasant job with everything polluted, filthy, and unsanitary. It happened that my office had also flooded so I would be working from home again until further notice.

I was not alone in this disaster. Thousands of homes had been flooded for a hundred miles around my house. The first responders were working for days without much sleep, along with thousands of volunteers. There were people traveling from as far away as Tennessee, Florida, and other states to lend a hand to all of us. It was an amazing experience to see so many people working together. Economic differences, racial issues, gender, religion, age, none of that got in the way of the goal, which was to aid their neighbors to move on with their lives.

After a few days, Darlene offered me a small apartment that she owned. It was currently empty and I could stay as long as I needed it, rent free. It was a perfect place for my dog and me to have a quiet place to stay and work. I reasoned that we would be there for a month or so.

What was I thinking? The flood was in August and we are about to begin the month of March. I am still in the apartment waiting for my house to be repaired. With so many houses damaged, the contractors were working non-stop to keep up. Supplies had to be ordered since this was so sudden and unexpected.

About six weeks after I settled into the apartment, I totaled my white Camry. It was about all I had left, and I loved it. I had had it for five years and it was almost paid for. My friend Connie helped me negotiate when I went to replace it and I bought a new red Camry. I don't love it yet, since I have car payments for several more years, but I am thankful to have it and good friends that give me a helping hand when I need them.

You may wonder why I am sharing all this. It's because of the abundant blessings and spiritual awareness I have received. Immediately I began to pray and ask God what I was to do. I had heard one of my daughters say during the cleanup, "We're moving fifty years of my mom's life onto the lawn." It was true. It would take pages to list the things I lost in the flood. I could fill pages with the wonderful things that have happened, also. I was reunited, either in person or some other method of contact, mail, email, phone calls, and more with friends and family that I had been separated from for years. Then I witnessed the love of mankind for one another. Best of all, the relationship with my children was on the mend.

One unexpected occurrence was the return of my grief for Dean. I was sure that my healing was nearing completion. My tears were fewer and I felt a joy that I had not felt in many years. Then it began, the tears, the praying for God to give him back to me, the dreams, the heartache was back. I went to the cemetery almost every day. I was miserable.

Why was I obsessing over him again? I tried to hide it from everyone, but Darlene picked up on it. We had been spending a lot of time together, mostly with her aiding me in the recovery from the flood. She and a friend that had guided me through the grief before, helped me see that whenever I couldn't deal with an issue I would return to my younger years, which included our life together and his death, thus the grief.

I am now on the road to recovery once again. I don't know if I will ever be completely over losing Dean, but God is revealing to me that He is the key to getting through my time in this world.

Epilogue

I AM CONVINCED, MORE THAN EVER, THAT GOD WANTED ME TO write this book at this time; His timing is always perfect. If anyone reads it or not, does not matter to me; it has done what it needed to do for a young Vietnam widow who has suffered with grief for the love of her life for more than fifty years. Though I know the healing is not complete, I give God all the glory for touching my heart, my mind, and my soul with his loving and healing hands.

There are four reasons I wrote this book:

The Fourth reason for this book is a partial account of the man who tried to rescue me from my sorrow and pain. He was jealous of my love for Dean and thought that pretending he didn't happen at all was the best way to help me. The first years were not good ones between us, but I grew to care for and understand him through our years together. He was my husband for twenty-nine years. He was a good man who loved me, and though I learned to love him, I could never give him the depth of love he wanted from me. My love for him was more than what I would feel for a close friend, but not what he wanted. I took care of his every need, as a wife should. He loved and cared for me and the children as a husband and father should. I learned to love him for who he was. He loved his son and daughters and his children adored him. People who knew him then still make comments about him being such a good and fun guy. People loved him.

He and I were very different. He loved to watch and play all sports and I knew only a little about baseball. I loved cars and music. He didn't know a carburetor from a radiator, and our taste in music was totally opposite. But with God's help, we made it work, through years of trials, tears, and determination.

We made a bad decision when we decided to get married so quickly. Different choices would have saved us a lot of heartaches, but there are no do overs in real life. There are consequences for everything we do. I would not have my precious children and grandchildren if we had made other choices. I am thankful to God and to Sam for them and for the man Sam became despite our problems.

Sam and I both believed that the Holy Bible is the word of God. We gave Him our lives and through the years we studied what God had to say to us through His word. One thing that became important to both of us is what God has to say about marriage. We studied it and talked about it, prayed together, and concluded that we were married for life, no matter what. We tried to follow God's instructions for marriage in the New Testament. *"Wives, submit yourselves to your own husbands as you do to the Lord."* Ephesians 5:22 and *"Husbands, love your wives, just as Christ loved the church and gave himself up for her that he might sanctify her...In this same way, husbands ought to love their wives as their own bodies. He who loves his wife loves himself."* Ephesians 5:25-26; and many other references to marriage throughout God's word.

Sam's greatest legacy is his children and grandchildren. I can see a part of him in each one of them. My family and friends asked me after Sam died if I would marry again. The answer was and is no. I have hurt too many people throughout my life because I made the decision to marry Sam when my heart was not free. Do I get lonely, some have asked? Yes, but I stay busy with my job, a variety of projects for my house, children, grandchildren, and friends, and my studies. I don't sit around and feel sorry for myself, though I have done that in the past.

The Third reason for this book is a record of my own personal healing experience. This book has been very emotional for me to write. Several times I had to set it aside for a few weeks or even years before I could continue. This time it became more than an emotional project for me after I found the pictures and my wedding band in my mother's house. It became a therapeutic obsession. I could not, *not* finish this book just as I cannot *not* love Dean.

God knew that I could not have done it any other way. I have spent more than fifty years trying to work through the grief. It was years filled with much fear, torment, and anger deep inside me. Fear of being left alone. Fear of my son going to war at some time in the future; Fear of the repercussions caused by our two first children being born the same month as Dean's birthday. Fear that someone would mention Dean's name around Sam. Fear of being insane and not knowing it. I can't help but think that if I had given myself time to grieve before remarrying; my life would have been easier, or at least very different. But then I may not have felt a need for God or learned to depend on Him as I have. Through all these experiences, God has truly become my Lord. He has continued to help me to be "anger free" and my focus is now on serving Him. I want to look more like Jesus in my words and actions and see heaven someday.

The Second reason for this book is for all the young Vietnam and other war widows or fiancés that I have had contact with through the Veterans' Group, those with whom I may meet one day, and those I may never know. If they were new to the military life, as I was, we had no support group of others like us, or at least not that most of us knew about. I'm afraid most of us were thrashing about just trying to make sense of what this war had done to our lives, present and future. No one I knew had any idea what I was experiencing, therefore, the advice I received was all wrong. I was sixteen years old with not much life experience to draw from. I truly believed he would come home to me and we would live happily ever after. I felt like some people around me thought I should just get over it. I heard things like, "He wouldn't want you to be so sad. And "You'll find someone else before you know it." Losing a husband this way was treated like any other death. The very composition of war makes it uncharacteristic of any other death. I have endured the death of a parent, grandparents, close friends, other family members, and my second husband; none of them were remotely like Dean's. Hopefully telling of my experience will help other young war widows not feel alone or at least be a comforting kind of strength to them. With confidence, I know it can give them *hope* by showing them what God can do with a shattered heart.

The First reason for this book is to document our love story; the love of my life, killed by small arms fire during Operation Pickett, a Search and Destroy mission in Kontum Province, Vietnam on January 10, 1967. Dean was trying to assist a brother soldier who had been hit by the same sniper's gun that killed them both.

Dean was proud to be a Screaming Eagle.

I have not included the few "*words of love*" that Dean wrote to me on the back of the pictures he sent to me. These are personal, and I can't make myself share them. I treasure each word.

This is a story of Alan Dean Whitlock from my perspective as a young wife deeply in love. Dean had a short life with no children or grandchildren to carry on for him, but I will be his legacy; I refuse to let him be forgotten. I gave him my heart when I was a thirteen-year-old girl and I have never owned it again to give away to another person. I tried for a while, to just not love him until I realized that it was impossible. It would be like not breathing. I have loved him, and he has been in my thoughts every day since that warm night in the summer of 1964 when we met.

June 7, 2016 would have been our fiftieth wedding anniversary and January 10, 2017 it was fifty years since he was killed. My love for Dean was so strong that it has been a continuing struggle for me to accept losing him. I still catch myself looking for him in the face of men who would be his age now; not expecting to see him, just trying to imagine how he would be. I have searched the internet on Vietnam War sites for his face or something relating to him. My heart still aches for him and the only thing I can think when he is heavy on my mind is, "I want him back, Lord," though I know it can't be.

Though I will always love and miss Dean and the life we planned, I live a good and contented life. I still have my job and I'm beginning to work out the differences with my children. They have given me six precious grandsons and one beautiful granddaughter. I have many friends and family members who love me, a small dog, and live in the country near my son and his family.

I feel that I have come full circle in these last years. I read a lot and write poetry, songs, and I'm starting a new book and have an idea for another one after that. Music is my constant companion again as it was when I was growing up. Sometimes I even fall asleep at night listening to my music. Victor Hugo said, "*Music expresses that which cannot be said and on which it is impossible to be silent."* I also read an anonymous quote that says, *"Music is what feelings sound like."* Another quote I love is *"Where Words Fail, Music Speaks."* I think these are perfect definitions of how essential music is, at least in my life. I still had some of the records we used to listen to; I would play them occasionally, until I lost them all in the flood.

I will always be grateful to Mr. Eric Clapton for his music. The words to his songs helped me define things I was feeling. It was like he understood, or at least whoever the lyricist was who penned the songs he recorded, had experienced the kind of pain and love that I felt. The emotion in which he sings touches my heart in a familiar way. His songs were not ones that Dean and I shared that make me sad when I hear them; they were new to me and expressed what I could not in my state of mind. I feel that this music saved my life, or at least my sanity, as the grief became unbearable. I would love to be able to thank Mr. Clapton and let him know what his songs have done for me. I cannot write music, so I had the music to one of his songs in my mind when I wrote the song for Dean.

God has blessed me, *"...exceedingly abundantly above all that we (I) ask or think, according to the power that works in us (me)."* (Ephesians 3:20). He has blessed me with people to love and precious memories. Who could ask for more?

I still take my memories to the cemetery every week or more and keep flowers on his and his mom's markers. At times, I still drive slowly through the small roads looking at the huge live oak trees and the hundreds of colors the flowers display among the perfectly manicured landscape. I think about all the friends and family I have known throughout my life that are now buried here. I usually drive past Jamie's grave and say, I love you my friend, for Dean and me. Always when I say goodbye to Dean before I leave the cemetery, I pause for a few minutes beside his grave, feeling the soft breeze on my face and in my hair before returning to my car. *"I will always love you,"* I whisper. I can almost hear him whispering softly in the wind, *"I love you, too, my Darling."*

I have been very lonely at times and will be until I die, because I am not with my beloved. No one else can fill that space. I gave my heart completely to only one man. Experience proves to me that my heart never has been and never will be free to love that way again.

How long does mourning last? I now know it can last an entire lifetime. I *know* that young love can also last a lifetime because a true love story has no end. Yes, I still shed a few tears at times when I hear a song that brings a special memory, or I think of the words he wrote to me. No love could be more passionate than mine for him. He lived…he loved… he was loved…he died…and he is still loved.

The following are some of my poems and songs written for him as I grieved through the years. Some are simple from a young heart and others from the heart of an older woman's memories.

Two weeks after we met, he already had my heart

Young Love (1984)

Many years have passed away,
Since youth caressed my face.
But the years vanish with just a thought,
Of kisses stolen in a secret place.
Many events have come and gone
Since my girlish deeds were done.
But memories are clear and fresh,
Of times shared with a special one.
Many people have touched my life
Since young love's gentle spark.
But feelings are so easily stirred
Of that young love within my heart.

Flowers (1984)

Beautiful colors beyond mere words,
Beautiful flowers, soft and real,
Gathered together with many emotions
With a love no one can kill.
Gathered for someone in the Silent Land,
Someone who is so precious to me
Given in love in a quiet place
To someone who cannot see.
Or maybe he knows of my longing heart,
Of my soul reaching out to him.
Maybe he knows the love I still feel
Though at times his face is dim.
Maybe he knows of my thoughts of him
I haven't forgotten his tender touch
Maybe he knows about the flowers
And that I still miss him so very much

153

His Other Woman (February 28, 2018)

There is another woman
Who holds him in her heart
Who thinks of him so often
When they must be apart
I wonder about her love for him
I'm sure it's just as strong,
As the love I have here in my heart?
Though I know I'm where he belongs.
He left so very long ago
He faces danger each day
Always he is in her prayers
Till he comes back this way
She misses him as I do
We both long to have him near
We wonder who he thinks about
As we are waiting here.
She and I share this fervent love
But it causes us no drama
For she is also in my heart
My Beloved, he calls her Momma

Faded Dreams (2016)

Sometimes I dream,
What might it have been like?
If you had survived the war
You left me to fight.
As you step off that plane
I run to greet you
Just as I have watched
Many other families do.
We laugh, and we cry
We hug, and we kiss
We must make up for
All the love we have missed.
You were scarred by the war
I watch and pray as you heal
I hold you at night
When the battles you feel.
You are still strong and brave
As the boy who went to war
But you come home a man
And I love you even more.
You look for work
Then go back to school
You find a good job
Where you can use your skills
We have a sweet daughter

Stephanie, as we'd planned
Then our little son arrives
Our precious Donovan
She has her daddy's eyes
And her momma's "red" hair
Like his dad, he has dark waves
Such a beautiful pair.
Then you surprise me
With your own plans
For our house you will build
With your own two hands
There is no need now
From your nightmares to heal
No plans need be drawn
For the house you would build.
The greeting with hugs and kisses
Will never come to be
And the beautiful children
We will never see.
Wonderful was the life
Made up in our faded dreams
But God's plan was different,
It seems.

My Last Breath — A song for Dean
(January 2017)

On the night we met,
I gave you my heart,
I've never wanted it back.
It's always been yours
On the day we were wed,
I promised my love,
Till the last beat of my heart,
Dying heart.
This promise that I made
With all that I am,
I would love you until
I've taken my last breath.
I've traveled down
Some lonely roads,
But my heart is yours forever
Ever yours.
Now you're gone
And I am left alone
But you still have my love
Till my last breath.
My last breath
I can't see you
In the silent land
Out of my sight

But still in my heart,
Faithful heart.
On the night we met,
I gave you my heart,
I've never taken it back.
It's always been yours
On the day we were wed,
I promised my love,
Till the last beat of my heart,
Dying heart.

My Guitar Man (2016)

I was there when you began to play
I was there when you learned the chords
I was there when you practiced your songs
I was there when you played for me
Then you went away, and I dreamed
Of the songs you sang to me
You promised that you would return
When you finished your responsibility
I waited anxiously for your return
With the music from your heart
I longed for your promised return
From the war that tore us apart.
I heard of you continuing to play
I yearned for your voice strong and clear
I heard of you getting better each day
Please bring your love for me to hear
I waited and waited for you
My ears hungered for your song
I listened and listened for you
But you were silent when you returned
Where are you my love?
Where are your promised songs?
Where is my guitar man?
You never returned to sing to me.

'Round And 'Round (November 20, 2017)

Memories go 'round and 'round in my mind
Tormenting and taunting my soul,
If only I could finally find
Relief and a peace I could hold
Music and melodies play in my thoughts
With every beat, my heart aches
Lyrics that were so meaningful to us
Each word that I hear, my heart breaks
Songs that in my ear you whispered
The way you teased, and you laughed
Your beautiful smile as you held me
They're gone a part of my past
Memories of our love haunts me
The things we used to do
Thoughts of your honey sweet kisses
Leave me longing for you
The tears I've cried each day and night
Fill my world with pain
There are no arms to comfort me
Just tears that fall like rain.

Sweet Memories (2017)

A memory of your touch
Brought a tear to my eye
Sadness was a part of me
I wanted to die
A thought of your smile
Also, made me weep
How I have missed you
Even in my sleep
In the pictures that you left
As I looked into your face
Anguish lived inside me
Made me long for your embrace
Please ease my pain
I begged God above
Help me to feel joy
When I think of our love
My sorrow went on and on
For many more years
In precious dreams of you
I'd awake with more tears
As I slowly learned
To listen to God's voice
I began to see clearly
Another, better choice
I studied God's Word

And continued to pray
My pain had decreased
I noticed on some days.
It took months of praying
And learning to hear
God's voice in my mind
He was easing my fear.
As I remembered your kisses
The things you would say
One day I saw a smile
Was gracing my face
O, God what a blessing
My memories could be
If I could, but smile
When his face I would see
The smile would appear
Appeared more often it seems
When those intimate memories
Escaped from my dreams
Thank you, My Father
When his love that I cherish
Returns in sweet memories
With no tears to tarnish.

Lord, You Healed My Heart (July 2017)
(written following my trip to Washington D.C.)

How do I say thank You,
For saving my sanity?
For answering my every prayer,
When I turned from humanity.
How do I express to others,
Your Magnificence and Glory?
I must for all my days
Relate to them my story.
How do I find the words?
I don't know how to start,
To tell of my anguish
And brokenness of my heart.
How did You take the pieces,
So, shattered by my grief,
Gently hold them in Your hands
Until I felt relief?
How did you dare to love me,
In my crushed and forlorn condition?
You healed my broken spirit
You *are* the Great Physician.
How did you calm the storm?
Raging inside my mind,
Ease the agony in my heart,
When no relief could I find?

Your resources are infinite.
You see with an eternal eye.
Your ways are not my ways.
Your ways are Most High.
You whispered to my loved ones,
You crooned to my friends.
You urged them to fervently pray.
You brought your strength to lend.
I could feel your arms around me as,
I stood before the Wall.
I heard you breathing softly,
"I have you, you will not fall."
I have no way to thank you, Lord.
You have blessed me immeasurably.
Your love is more than I deserve.
I will praise You throughout eternity?

About The Author

BJ COLEMAN BEGAN WRITING POETRY AS A YOUNG WOMAN. SHE was presented with an opportunity to publish a few of her works and given another opportunity to write articles for a Christian woman magazine. Her passion was writing, but her reality was that she had four children to raise. She was a stay-at-home mom until they finished high school. At 46, her children gone and recently widowed for the second time, she enrolled in a computer class and some writing classes, where she was encouraged by her instructors to write her memoirs, if only for her own pleasure. It seemed God had other plans for her writing. Through a series of events, her story evolved into a book she wanted to share with anyone who was dealing with grief in an extreme way: especially those affected by war.

BJ also manages a Facebook group of people who have been lost in their grief for many years. It is a support group that encourages healing from grief. She is an amateur blogger on her website, bjcolemanwriter. com, where visitors can subscribe to learn about her book release and her latest book, a work of fiction based on fact about dealing with adoption.

CPSIA information can be obtained
at www.ICGtesting.com
Printed in the USA
FFHW021458301018
49003925-53254FF

9 781947 309470